The Mystery of
MANNA

The Psychedelic Sacrament of the Bible

DAN MERKUR

Park Street Press
Rochester, Vermont

Park Street Press
One Park Street
Rochester, Vermont 05767
www.InnerTraditions.com

Park Street Press is a division of Inner Traditions International

Library of Congress Cataloging-in-Publication Data

Merkur, Daniel.
    The mystery of manna : the psychedelic sacrament of the Bible / Dan Merkur.
        p.   cm.
    Includes bibliographical references and index.
    ISBN 0-89281-772-0 (alk. paper)
    1. Manna. 2. Hallucinogenic drugs and religious experience—History. 3. Drugs in the Bible. 4. Ergot. I. Title.
    BS1245.5.M47 1999
    291.4'2—dc21   99-42800
                                                      CIP

Printed and bound in Canada

10 9 8 7 6 5 4 3 2 1

This book was typeset in Caslon with Caslon Antique as the display typeface

Contents

Preface

*I*n *The Road to Eleusis,* R. Gordon Wasson, Carl A. P. Ruck, and Albert Hofman, argued "that the Eleusinian Mysteries, and probably the other mystery religions of classical Greece, can be interpreted as communal shamanic seances, in which mystical visionary experience was induced by the ingestion of drugs. For the Greater Eleusinian Mystery, the drug was a water-soluble extract of ergot."[1] This book argues that in Israel, too, the psychedelics in ergot were the sacrament of a mystery tradition. As I shall show, knowledge of the biblical mystery was preserved as a secret as late as the thirteenth century.

This study is intended as a contribution to the history of religion. I have made no attempt to write an exhaustive history; to do so would require a complete survey of the literature of Judaism and Christianity, seeking usually brief passages that allude to the mystery of manna. Such a project would require the collaboration of specialists in many areas of research. Similarly, I have not known where to begin to investigate the possibility of the mystery's transmission to Islam. Here it must suffice to make a beginning by placing the topic in the public domain.

I have limited my discussion, so far as possible, to texts that openly discuss the mystery in explicit statements. These statements usually consist of a single clause, sentence, or motif that, the authors trusted, casual readers would overlook, misunderstand, or refuse to treat seriously. When the evidence is equivocal, so that a historical author may or may not have known of the mystery, I have usually not included a discussion in this book. To this rule I have made only three exceptions, all in chapter 9, and I have indicated them accordingly.

ONE

Manna and the Showbread

*T*his book is about a secret. The biblical story of manna, the miraculous bread that God sent the Israelites in the wilderness, has been interpreted by several of the most illustrious authorities in both Judaism and Christianity in a consistent manner that none of us is taught publicly. The secret exegetical tradition associated the Israelites' consumption of manna "in the morning" (Exod. 16:8, 12) with their vision of the glory of God, also "in the morning" (Exod. 16:7).

The historical existence of an esoteric interpretation of manna is, I shall demonstrate, a fact that even the most skeptical examination of the evidence must acknowledge. Why the interpretation was made and why it was kept secret, or at least partially secret, are questions whose answers are not in evidence.

For the historian of religion, a secret is like a crossword puzzle. Historical research can describe the age, size, shape, and wording of the clues of the puzzle. It can describe the ink, the paper, and the font. What a historian most wants to know, however, the correct solution of the puzzle, is not attested. The solution can be hypothesized, but it cannot be proved. Still, if progress is to be made, it is necessary to resort to hypothesis—call it theory, speculation, guesswork, as you wish—to cover the gap in the data.

To account for the empirical fact of the interpretive tradition that emphasized manna's association with visions of the glory, I propose that the biblical story of manna received its distinctive interpretation among Jewish and Christian exegetes who recognized the relevance of manna to the practice of visionary mysticism. More precisely, by stating that when the Israelites ate manna they envisioned the glory of God, the Bible plainly and openly claimed that manna was what we would today call "psychoactive." Eating manna facilitated the occurrence of a vision, and many prominent Jewish and Christian religious authorities over the centuries have secretly known that it did so.

They kept their knowledge secret because, among other reasons, they did not wish to be ridiculed, shunned, vilified, or violently persecuted for their religious beliefs.

Let us proceed immediately to examine the historical data. There are two unequivocal references to the psychoactive properties of manna in the Hebrew Bible. The first occurs in the compendium[1] of manna narratives in Exodus 16. The relevant verses read:

> So Moses and Aaron said to all the children of Israel, "At evening you shall know that Yahveh made you go out of the land of Egypt, and in the morning you shall see the glory of Yahveh. . . . When Yahveh gives you
>
> > 'Meat to eat in the evening,
> > and bread to the full in the morning,'
>
> because Yahveh has heard your murmurings which you murmur against him—for what are we? Your murmurings are not against us but against Yahveh." Then Moses said to Aaron, "Say to the whole congregation of the children of Israel, 'Come near before Yahveh, for he has heard your murmurings.'" And it was as Aaron had spoken to the whole congregation of the children of Israel. They looked toward the wilderness, and behold, the glory of Yahveh appeared in the cloud. (Exod. 16:6–7a, 8b–10)[2]

In the morning, when the Israelites were to eat the manna, Aaron told them to approach Yahveh. Later in the biblical narrative, after the ark of the covenant had been built, the phrase "approach Yahveh" might have referred to approaching the mercy seat atop the ark. In Exodus 16, however, the ark did not yet exist, and the phrase referred to Yahveh's presence. Moreover, the remark implied that by eating manna, the Israelites would enter Yahveh's presence. And so they did! They did not move spatially, however. They merely looked out toward the desert and had visions of the glory of Yahveh.

For the Priestly (P) author writing in the late eighth century as part of Hezekiah's reformation,[3] "glory" was a technical theological term that referred to the visible form that represented Yahveh in dreams and prophetic visions.[4] Theological views differed concerning the nature of the manifest phenomenon. Yahveh's glory was sometimes conceived as a glamour or aura emitted by his person, but at other times as a hypostasis or an independent angel. At the opposite extreme, the glory was sometimes understood as an anthropomorphic mental image that accompanied, and was envisioned as speaking the words, of Yahveh's revelation. Whatever nuance the Priestly writer intended in his concept of Yahveh's glory, his text is unequivocal that eating manna was the occasion of a vision of Yahveh's glory. Manna was a psychoactive substance; its ingestion induced religious experiences.[5]

The psychoactivity of manna is consistent with two distinctive claims of the legend of Moses. Exodus 16 asserts that all of the Israelites saw the glory at the same time. What is more, Moses announced the time of the Israelites' religious experiences in advance of their occurrence. These features of the work of Moses were duplicated, several chapters later, when all of Israel heard Yahveh speak the Ten Commandments at Mount Sinai; and they have been much emphasized in Jewish commentaries on the Mosaic covenant. On the other hand, similar circumstances are extremely rare in the general history of religions. Historical research knows of only two means by which a large mass of people may have religious experiences simultaneously: mass hysteria, and psychoactive drug use. A moderately sized group, all within earshot of each other, may make use of hypnotic states; but the biblical legend of Moses specifically excluded the possibility of hypnotic suggestion, for example, when the elders Eldad and Medad were described as prophesying in the camp, out of the presence of Moses (Num. 12:26–27). Moreover, because it is not possible to predict the specific time of the onset of hysterical spells and fugues, the legend of Moses cannot be reconciled with a hypothesis of mass hysteria. Hysteria is too unreliable for the purpose of a ritual event that is held on a previously determined date and time. Psychoactive drug use is the only viable explanation for the biblical legend of Moses' introduction of the entire adult population of Israel into the visual and verbal revelations of Yahveh.

The second biblical passage that refers explicitly to the psychoactivity of manna occurs in Isaiah. The text reads: "And my Lord will give you the bread of hardship and the water of affliction, and your Teacher will no longer hide himself, and your eyes shall see your Teacher" (Isa. 30:20). The composition of this verse in prose within a passage that is otherwise poetry indicates that it was an interpolation by a later editor. Another indication of its secondary character is its concern not with the politics of Isaiah's era but with the end times. In amplification of the hope for universal prophetism in Num. 11:29 and Joel 3:1, the editor associated manna with visions of God in the future era of Israel's redemption. The reference to manna as "the bread of hardship" is consistent, however, with the negative criticism of manna in Num. 11:4–9.

Beyond these two references, I have found no further references to a psychoactive sacrament in the Hebrew Bible that are explicit, conclusive, and inarguable.[6]

The Bread of the Presence

There is, however, an abundance of biblical material, previously obscure, that becomes comprehensible when manna is understood to have been psychoactive. These passages provide sufficient detail that manna may be botanically identified with reasonable confidence.

Different passages in Exodus 16 reflect different attitudes to the availability of manna. In verse 32, Moses reported Yahveh's commandment that an omer of manna be on permanent display to the people of Israel. In verses 33 and 34, by contrast, Moses instructed Aaron to put an omer of manna in a jar in front of the ark of the covenant in the tabernacle, where none might enter but a priest. The first version, deriving from the Yahwist (J) source document in the tenth century B.C.E., advocated public knowledge of manna and reflects a practice that dates to early in the history of biblical Israel. The second version, composed by the Priestly (P) author, instead restricted access to manna to the priesthood.

What did Jerusalem's priests do to fulfill the commandment to keep manna on display? Or, to put the question another way: What among the ritual objects of Solomon's temple was described in biblical narrative as manna?

The answer is not far to seek. According to Josh. 5:11–12, unleavened bread was substituted in Canaan for the manna of the wilderness years.

> And they ate of the produce of the land on the morrow after the Passover, unleavened bread and parched grain on that very day. And the manna ceased on the morrow, when they ate of the produce of the land. The people of Israel had manna no more, but ate of the fruit of the land of Canaan that year.

Immediately after the Israelites crossed the Jordan River and ate the produce of Canaan, Yahveh ceased to provide them with manna. Unleavened bread replaced manna in their diet. Interestingly, the Israelites did not eat the produce of Canaan on their first night in Canaan. They crossed the Jordan on the tenth of the spring month (Josh. 4:19) and it is implied that they ate manna with the Passover sacrifice on the fourteenth of the month,[7] since they only substituted unleavened bread for manna after the Passover, that is, during the week-long Feast of Unleavened Bread that began on the fifteenth of the month (Lev. 23:6).

Was Joshua's Passover anciently regarded as a unique event of the legendary past? Or was Passover once a traditional time for the consumption of psychoactive sacraments? We cannot answer these questions. The legend of Joshua suggests, however, that biblical legends discussed manna as a literary poeticizing of living ritual practice that concerned the unleavened bread that was placed on a table in the holy of holies, or outer part of the inner chamber of Solomon's temple in front of the ark.

The parallels between manna and the showbread were extensive. The location of manna "before Yahveh" in Exod. 16:33–34 is identical to the location of "the holy bread . . . the bread of the Presence" (1 Sam. 21:6) that was placed "before Yahveh" (Lev. 24:8) on a table in the holy place of the tabernacle (Exod. 25:23–30; Lev. 24:1–9). Pro forma a sacrifice to Yahveh, for consumption by Yahveh and his angelic attendants, the showbread might reasonably have been called "the bread of angels" (Ps. 78:25); but the phrase in Psalm 78 was appropriate to showbread, not to manna. Again, the description of manna in Exod. 16 tends to suggest the bread of the Presence. The manna was "a fine, flake-like thing, fine as hoarfrost on the earth" (16:14b). In other words, manna had the form of a flaky pastry or biscuit. Because the bread of the Presence was "a most holy portion out of the offerings by fire to Yahveh" (Lev. 24:9), it was required to be unleavened: "No cereal offering which you bring to Yahveh shall be made with leaven; for you shall burn no leaven nor any honey as an offering by fire to Yahveh" (Lev. 2:11). This statute helps explain the priests' obligation to eat the showbread on the Sabbath, a full week after it was baked (Lev. 24:8-9). Leavened bread would have been stale and moldy;[8] unleavened bread was still edible. Although unleavened, the showbread was a kind of pastry. Ezekiel listed its ingredients as "fine flour and oil and honey" (16:19). Manna similarly tasted like "cakes baked with oil" (Num. 11:8). Again, it was "white, and the taste of it was like wafers made with honey" (Exod. 16:31b). The only ingredient of manna that was not paralleled in the surviving recipes of the bread of the Presence was its description as being "like coriander seed" (Exod.

16:31b). The quantities are in agreement, however. In both the J and P legends, one omer of manna was to be kept as a memorial (Exod. 16:32, 33); and "an omer is the tenth part of an ephah" (Exod. 16:36). In addition, the Israelites gathered an omer of manna daily, excepting the sixth day when they gathered a double portion that was to last them through the Sabbath (Exod. 16:22). Similarly, in the Priestly code, each cake of the bread of the Presence was to be made of "two-tenths of an ephah" (Lev. 24:5) of flour. In other words, like the Sabbath gathering of manna, the Sabbath bread of the Presence was two omers in quantity. Indeed, Jews to this day place two loaves of sweet bread at table on Sabbath eve in commemoration of the manna.

What little we know of the history of the showbread compares with the history of manna. The ritual, cultic use of the bread of the Presence antedated Solomon's temple. It is attested as a Gibeonite practice at Nob in the era of David. When David fled the court of Saul and came to Ahimelech, a priest of the dynasty of Eli at the shrine of Nob, David asked for bread to eat.

> "Now then, what have you under your hand? Give to my hand five loaves of bread, or whatever is here." And the priest answered David, and said, "There is no common bread under my hand, but only holy bread. If only the young men had guarded themselves against women!" And David answered the priest, and said, "But women have been kept from us as always when I go out [to battle]. And the vessels of the young men shall be holy. If it is [in] a common way, then today it shall be holy in the vessel." So the priest gave him holy [bread]; for there was no bread there but the bread of the Presence, which is removed from before Yahveh, to be replaced by hot bread on the day it is taken away. (1 Sam. 21:4–6)

Just as manna was once on public display, David saw and was permitted to eat the bread of the Presence at Nob. Ahimelech was concerned that the young warriors and their eating utensils be ritually clean, but otherwise he had no hesitation about giving the showbread to laypeople. Centuries later, the Priestly author relocated both the manna and the bread of the Presence within the holy place of the sanctuary, where priests alone had access to them. In both cases, the practices concerning manna corresponded to what were then the current rules in regard to the bread of the Presence. It is highly probable, then, that the biblical accounts of manna were origin legends of the bread of the Presence.

It may be argued, of course, that the showbread was a nonpsychoactive substitute for manna, as Passover *matzot* have traditionally been; but if so, why was the bread of the Presence "unique among the grain-offerings in being an integral part, not of the sacrificial ritual of the court, but of the rites performed inside the tabernacle"?[9] Conversely, if the showbread was not psychoactive, why did the Priestly author associate the ingestion of manna with the vision of the glory of Yahveh? There is no avoiding the conclusion that a psychoactive substance that was euphemistically called "manna" in biblical legend was known by P to be available "before Yahveh" in Solomon's temple.

The term *man*, "manna," is no aid in identifying the substance. Exod. 16:15 derives the term as a play on the word *what?* When the Israelites said, "What *(man)* is it?," they inadvertently named it. Because Hebrew grammar permits *man hu* to be understood to mean both "What is it?" and "It is what," the Israelites opted for the wordplay and came jokingly to call it "what." What they called it when they were not joking, the Bible does not say. Manna's identity—like that of the runner on second base—was evidently a riddle.

If the psychoactive cult object that was euphemistically called manna was not the showbread, it was something else. Under the circumstances, the many parallels between manna and the showbread make the bread of the Presence by far the most probable candidate.

On the other hand, there was certainly some variation in the significance of the term *manna*. Insofar as manna weighed an omer or two, the term referred to an entire cake of unleavened bread. The Priestly author, however, referred instead to a substance that might be either baked or boiled (Exod. 16:23). P presumably intended an ingredient that was added to the bread of the Presence and consumed when the bread was eaten. Because the ingredient imbued the pastry with its properties, the connotation and practical implication of the term *manna* were unaffected by variations in its references to the bread and its psychoactive ingredient.

The Draught Ordeal

The association of "the bread of hardship and the water of affliction" with the vision of God in Isa. 30:22 is explained by the two accounts of the draught ordeal in Num. 5:11–31. Like the showbread, the draught ordeal was categorized as a cereal offering.

The extant text of Num. 5:11–31 is apparently an editorial interweaving of two statutes.[10] The first governed the case of a woman publicly believed to be an adulteress (Num. 5:11–13); the second governed the case of a woman whose husband only suspected her of adultery (Num. 5:14). In the first case,

> the priest shall take holy water in an earthen vessel, and take some of the dust that is on the floor of the tabernacle and put it into the water. And the priest shall set the woman before Yahveh, and loose the woman's head [hair], and place in her hands the offering of memory, which is the offering of jealousy. . . . Then let the priest make the woman take the oath of the execration, and say to the woman, "Yahveh shall give you over to [the effects of] an execration and an oath in the midst of your people, when Yahveh makes your thigh drop [off] and your stomach swell." . . . And the priest shall take the offering of jealousy out of the woman's hand, and shall wave the offering before Yahveh and bring it to the altar; and the priest shall take a handful of the cereal offering, as its memorial portion, and sacrifice it on the altar. Afterward he shall make the woman drink the water. When he has made her drink the water . . . the woman shall be [given over] to an execration in the midst of her people. (Num. 5:17–18a, 21, 25–27a, 27c)

In this statute, the dust on the floor of the tabernacle in the inner sanctum "before Yahveh" (Num. 5:17–18) was assumed to be toxic. On the conventional assumption that the floor of the tabernacle was a projection into the era of Moses of the floor of the Jerusalem temple, the concern with a cereal offering suggests the sort of dust that would have been found on the threshing floor of Araunah, which the Jerusalem sanctuary had once been. Implicitly, dust such as would have been left on a floor where grain was threshed was added to holy water. The accused woman was ritually cursed and made to drink the poisoned water. Because she was guilty, she would become severely ill.

The interwoven verses presented another statute that governed the case of a woman who might be innocent.

> And the priest shall bring her near, and have her stand before Yahveh. . . . And in his hands the priest shall have the bitter water that curses. Then the priest shall make her take an oath, saying to the woman, "If no man has lain with you, and if you have not deviated into corruption under your husband, be clean of this bitter water that curses. But if you have gone astray under your husband, and if you have become corrupt, and a man has lain with you other than your husband . . . may this bitter water that curses come into your bowels and make your stomach swell and your thigh drop [off]." And the woman shall say, "Amen, Amen." Then the priest shall write these execrations in a book, and erase them into the bitter water; and he shall make the woman drink the bitter water that curses, and the bitter waters that curse shall enter her. . . . Then, if she has become corrupt and has acted unfaithfully against her husband, the bitter water that curses shall enter into her, and her stomach shall swell and her thigh drop [off]. But if the woman has not become corrupt, but is pure, then she shall be clean and be able to conceive children. (Num. 5:16, 18b–20, 22-24a, 27b–28)

This statute presupposed that toxic water had already been prepared. The priest brought the water to the woman and cursed her. When she accepted the curse, it was written down and the ink was washed into the toxic water. The toxins were thus magically associated with the words of the curse, before the woman drank. The outcome of the drink was variable. If the woman was guilty, she suffered bitter pain and severe illness; if not, not.[11]

The toxic dust that was taken from threshing floors and mixed with water for the cereal offering of the draught ordeal may be identified with confidence as ergot *(Claviceps purpurea)*, a fungus that infests the grains of barley, wheat, rye, and other cereal grasses.[12] Cases of ergot poisoning take form either as *Ergotismus gangraenosus*, or, if complicated by vitamin A deficiency,[13] as *Ergotismus convulsivus*. Barger stated that "symptoms common to both types are vomiting, a feeling of intense heat or cold, pain in the muscles of the calf, the yellow colour of the face, the formation of vesicles on the hands and feet . . . severe diarrhoea (often a precursor of death) and some impairment of mental function."[14] Additionally, in gangrenous ergotism,

> the part affected (more often a foot than a hand) becomes somewhat swollen and inflamed. . . . A feeling of intense heat alternated with one of icy cold. . . . Gradually the part affected became numb. . . . Later the diseased part became black, often quite suddenly. . . . The gangrenous part shrank, became mummified and dry; the whole body was emaciated and the gangrene gradually spread upwards. . . . The separation of the gangrenous part often took place spontaneously at a joint without pain or loss of blood. . . . The extent of the gangrene varied from the mere shedding of nails, and the loss of fingers and toes . . . to that of whole limbs.[15]

The initial swelling and loss of gangrenous extremities were the chief symptoms noted by the Priestly code.[16]

The draught ordeal depended on ergot's toxicity. The association of manna with the draught ordeal in Isa. 30:22, since both produced visions of God, referred instead to ergot's psychoactivity. The psychedelic factors in ergot are lysergic acid amides, the organic psychoactive substances from which d-lysergic acid diethylamide (LSD-25) is synthesized.

Honey from a Rock

J's account of the Israelites' rebellion over the waters of Marah, "which means bitter," becomes comprehensible in view of the potentially fatal toxins of "the bitter waters that curse." The legend is set immediately prior to the manna narratives.

> When they came to Marah, they could not drink the waters of Marah because they were bitter. That is why its name was called Marah ["Bitter"]. The people murmured against Moses, saying, "What shall we drink?" So he cried to Yahveh, and Yahveh showed him a tree. When he threw [it] into the water, the water became sweet. There he made them a statute and a judgment and there he tried them, saying, "None of the diseases that I put on the Egyptians will I put on you; for . . . Yahveh is your healer." (Exod. 15:23–26a, 26c)

Both Wellhausen and Bantsch believed that Exod. 15:25b contains an archaic account of the Mosaic covenant that located the epoch-making event at Marah rather than at Sinai.[17] J likely mentioned a tree for two reasons: to allude to his tale of the trees in Eden, which I shall review in the next chapter, and because ergot bears a small crimson psychedelic fruit that has the characteristic treelike shape of a mushroom.[18]

In the version of the legend of Moses that scholars attribute to the Elohist (E) source, both the miraculous provision of water and the Mosaic covenant were located at Mount Horeb, where Moses hit the rock and water came out of it (Exod. 17:1–7). The motif of a rod or staff, which replaced J's reference to a tree, was derived from the common desert practice, accurately portrayed in Num. 21:16–18, of using a staff to poke through the earth to create a well.[19] Its use to break through stone was anomalous. E, however, drew on a motif, first found in the poetry of the Song of Moses (Deut. 32), that had referred to the ingredients of the showbread emerging from a rock: "and he suckled him on honey from a crag, / and oil out of the rock" (Deut. 32:13).

Psalm 81:17 similarly refers to the ingredients of the bread of the Presence: "And he would feed him with the white of wheat, / and with honey from a rock I would satisfy you."

P followed E's version with its miraculous provision of water. P set the event after the covenant and located it at Kadesh (Num. 20:1–13). Kadesh is commonly identified with Ain Qadis, one of whose four main springs "flows out of a rock in three jets, each as thick as a man's arm."[20] The spring at Kadesh may have inspired the transformation of the motif of sweetening bitter water into the motif of water flowing out of a rock; but the source of an image should never be confused with the meaning that was used to convey it.

Moses "tried," "proved," or "tested" the Israelites at Marah (Exod. 15:25b) by a procedure closely related to the ritual trial by ordeal to which women accused of adultery were subjected. Because the waters later became sweet (15:25a), it is clear that the term *marim* was intended, as it has traditionally been understood, to convey the sense of "bitter." Driver has argued, however, that the term should instead be derived, not from *mar*, "bitter," but from the noun *mareh*, "disputed," "rebellious," through an assumed verb-root, *mari*, "to rebel, dispute, contend."[21] Exod. 15:23 would then be translated, "When they came to Rebellion, they could not drink the waters of rebellion, because they were rebellious. That is why its name was called Rebellion." We may well imagine that the Israelites objected to Moses' request that they consume the very substance whose toxins were used in trials by ordeal. Certainly it was because the "bitter waters" were popularly expected to cause the body to bloat and limbs to drop off that Moses was obliged to assure the Israelites that they would not suffer disease because Yahveh was their healer.

How did Moses sweeten the bitter waters? According to Hofmann, "lysergic acid amide, lysergic acid hydroxyethylamide, and ergonovine, are soluble in water, in contrast to the non-hallucinogenic . . . alkaloids of the ergotamine and ergotoxine type. With the techniques and equipment available in antiquity it was therefore easy to prepare an hallucinogenic extract from suitable kinds of ergot."[22] The psychedelic factors in ergot are water soluble, but the uterotonic factors are not. The draught ordeal was dangerous because solid vegetable matter was consumed along with the water. The sweet waters of Marah were safe because only water and water-soluble psychedelics were swallowed.

In this context, Moses' sweetening of the waters by means of a tree may be treated as a metaphor that was consistent with the assertion in Deut. 32:13 that Yahveh suckled Israel on "honey from a rock." The rock formation was the stony spur of ergot. When water came out of it, the honey of manna flowed. The waters of Marah and manna were different motifs pertaining to a single event in the legend of Moses: the sacramental administration of psychedelics at the covenant with God.[23]

The Quantity of Manna

Many readers treat the physically impossible miracle stories of the Bible at face value. For some, the stories are historical accounts of supernatural events. For others, the tales are evidence either of the naive credulity of biblical authors, or of their pious fraud. My own approach differs. In keeping with research by folklorists on the genre termed a "belief-legend,"[24] I generally treat stories of the impossible as symbolic or metaphoric expressions of the possible.

The miraculous capacity of manna to satiate, in all quantities great or small, may be understood not as a fabulous motif, but as a straightforward discussion of the recommended dosage. "This is what Yahveh has commanded: 'Gather of it, every man according to what he eats.' The children of Israel did so. They gathered, some more, some less. . . . He that gathered much had nothing over, and he that gathered little had no lack. Each had gathered according to what he ate" (Exod. 16:16-18).[25]

No matter how little or how much people gathered and consumed, they ate neither too little nor too much. Apparently, a very small quantity of manna sufficed to produce the desired visionary state, while an overdose was impossible. Although data is not available concerning naturally occurring lysergic amides, the parallel with the much more potent synthetic LSD is precise. Ott states: "There is no danger of death or injury from overdose of LSD. . . . No human being has ever died from an overdose of LSD

... the drug is not at all toxic. The danger ... is of experiencing a more intense effect than one is prepared for."[26]

Another "miracle" story with the same significance was told of the prophet Elijah. When Elijah visited a widow in Zarephath, he asked for bread (1 Kings 17:8–11), only to receive a strange reply.

> But when she said, "As Yahveh your God lives, I have nothing baked, only a handful of meal in a jar, and a little oil in a cruse; and now, I am gathering a couple of sticks, that I may go in and prepare it for myself and my son, that we may eat it, and die." Elijah said to her, "Do not fear! Come, do as you have said. Only make me a little cake of it first, and bring it out to me, and make for yourself and your son afterward. For so says Yahveh the God of Israel, 'The jar of meal shall not be finished, and the cruse of oil shall not lack, until the day that Yahveh sends rain upon the earth.'" And she went and did as Elijah said; and he, and she, and her household ate for days. The jar of meal did not finish, nor did the cruse of oil lack, according to the word of Yahveh which he spoke by the hand of Elijah. (1 Kings 17:12–16)

Like manna, the meal and oil remained effective even in minute quantities. Although the motif of a never-ending food supply is a folkloristic commonplace with no necessary association to psychoactive substances, the interwoven motifs in the legend of Elijah bear noting. When the widow proposed to bake meal and oil, so as to eat and die, Elijah told her to have no fear, because he would eat the cake first. In the sequel, Elijah and the widow were fine; but because the widow's son died, Elijah was obliged to facilitate his resurrection (1 Kings 17:17–24). These motifs of death and resurrection are comprehensible in terms of a well-known variety of psychedelic experiences that have variously been termed "death-rebirth" experiences, "ego-death," "acute panic states," and, by Grof, "perinatal matrix IV."[27] Equivalent experiences may also be induced through sensory depression and visualization and are known in historical studies as "ecstatic death," "mystic death," and "initiatory death."[28] The experiences consist of acute anxiety attacks that are attended by intense and frequently visual fantasies of dying. Both the attacks and the attendant fantasies may end abruptly, leading one to think one has survived death.[29] Prophetic legends conceptualized this type of experience as death and resurrection.

Ophrah and Jerusalem

Because the draught ordeal made a cereal offering of dust that was taken specifically from the floor of a threshing room, it may be pertinent that two biblical legends describe threshing floors as the locations of ecstatic visions. Both visions were celebrated, first by the establishment of altars on the threshing floors, and later by the construction of permanent sanctuaries on the sites.[30]

Gideon was threshing grain at the time of his initial encounter with an angel of Yahveh, and he erected an altar at the place. Once the editorial interpolations of Judg. 6:13–18[31] are deleted, the archaic narrative reads as follows.

> Now an angel of Yahveh came and sat under the oak at Ophrah, which belonged to Joash the Abiezerite, as his son Gideon was threshing wheat in the winepress, to hide it from the Midianites. When the angel of Yahveh appeared to him, he said to him, "Yahveh is with you, hero of arms.". . . So Gideon came over and made a goat kid and unleavened bread from an ephah of flour. The meat he put in a basket, and the broth he put in a pot. Then he brought them out to him under the oak and presented them. The angel of God said to him, "Take the meat and the unleavened bread, and rest them on this rock. Then pour out the broth." So he did so. Then the angel of Yahveh reached out the tip of the staff that was in his hand, and touched the meat and the unleavened bread; and there went up fire from the rock and it consumed the meat and the unleavened bread; and the angel of Yahveh went from his sight. When Gideon saw that he was an angel of Yahveh, Gideon said, "Ahah! my lord Yahveh! For I have seen an angel of Yahveh face to face." But Yahveh said to him, "Peace be to you. Do not fear; you shall not die." Then Gideon built an altar there to Yahveh, and called it, "Yahveh of Peace." To this day it is still at Ophrah of the Abiezerites. (Judg. 6:11–12,19–24)

Gideon's dismay, "Ahah! my lord Yahveh!", in verse 22 indicates that he had not realized that his visitor was an angel until after the angel's departure. The visitor evidently looked, to all appearances, like an ordinary man. So far as Gideon had known, the man had happened by and greeted him with a blessing. Gideon had then extended hospitality by preparing a meal for his visitor. Since Gideon was at work threshing grain and may not have had any yeast at hand, his preparation of unleavened bread does not necessarily imply any ritual intention.

The rare word *mis'enet,* "staff," has the sense of a walking stick in Exod. 21:19 and Zech. 8:4. In Num. 21:8, where it is juxtaposed with "scepter," the term refers instead to a small ceremonial staff that was an insignia of royal office. In the latter sense, Rabshakeh, commander of an Assyrian army, referred to Pharaoh as "the broken reed of a staff" (2 Kings 18:21; Isa. 36:6); and Ezekiel criticized Pharaoh as "a staff of reed" (Ezek. 29:6). Psalms 23:4 makes metaphoric use of the term in reference to Yahveh's sovereignty: "your rod and your staff, they shall comfort me." The word otherwise occurs in the Bible to designate the staff of Elisha, which Elisha's servant Gehazi employed in an unsuccessful attempt to revive the Shunammite's son from death (2 Kings 4:29, 32). The miraculous powers that were attributed to Elisha's staff suggest that something other than either a walking staff or an insignia of royal office was intended. Gideon's angelic visitor was said to have used his staff in a manner that alluded to Moses' action in striking his rod on a rock at Horeb, which caused the rock to produce water (Exod. 17:6 and parallels). At the same time, the consumption of a sacrifice by a miraculous fire was a traditional motif that signified its acceptance by God (Gen. 15:17; Lev. 9:24; 2 Kings 1:10, 12). Since the showbread was a cereal offering, the blending of motifs was appropriate. In Gideon's legend, both the allusion to Moses' rod and the motif that something came out of a rock served to indicate that Gideon's visitor was responsible for making their meal psychoactive.

Conventional interpretations infer that as soon as the fire

emerged from the rock and consumed the food, the angel vanished, and Gideon realized that his visitor had been an angel. Gideon's fear for himself and Yahveh's reassuring reply are then both unanticipated and unexplained. The text is less puzzling, however, when the time sequence is understood differently. Although the visitor's staff caused fire to emerge from the rock, the fire did not emerge, and Gideon did not recognize his visitor as an angel, until after the angel had left his sight. There is no textual obstacle to an understanding that Gideon entered an alternate psychic state in consequence of the visitor's actions, but did not recognize his ecstasy as such until after his visitor had departed. What was at stake in this detail was whether ecstasy was induced, as by Moses (Num. 12:26–27) and Samuel (1 Sam. 19:23), in the absence of a teaching prophet; or instead required a spiritual guide's presence, since it was produced through heterohypnosis, as by the false prophet Zedekiah, son of Chananiah (1 Kings 22:24). Gideon's ecstasy was of a type that warranted allusion to the Moses legend. Whether it involved visual phenomena is uncertain. It definitely involved prophetic dialogue with Yahveh.

So understood, the tale provides no indication that the angel was other than an ordinary human being. Since Gideon did not realize that the visitor had been an angel until after the angel had departed, the visitor may have "left his sight" in a manner consistent with human actions. He may very well have gotten up and walked away. Indeed, the term *mal'ak* is perhaps better understood here in its literal sense, "messenger," than in its secondary and figurative sense, "angel." The legend describes Gideon's prophetic initiation by a man whom he regarded as a "messenger of Yahveh." The man touched his "staff" to Gideon's food, causing the food to become psychoactive.

The legend of Gideon also contains a number of further motifs that warrant consideration in this connection. It was on a threshing floor that Gideon first attempted to divine (Judg. 6:36–40). Again, when Gideon entered the camp of the Midianites,

Amalekites, and people of the east, he overheard the discussion of a dream about mold-infested barley bread.

> When Gideon came, behold, a man was telling a dream to his comrade; and he said, "Behold, I dreamed a dream. And behold! a moldy barley bread tumbled into the camp of Midian, and came up to the tent, and hit it so that it fell, and turned it over, so that the tent collapsed." And his comrade answered, and said, "This is no other than the sword of Gideon the son of Joash, a man of Israel; into his hand God has given Midian and all the camp." (Judg. 7:13–14)

Because ergot is a fungus that infests barley, among other grains, the reference specifically to a moldy barley cake leaves little room for misunderstanding. The designation of the moldy cake as "the sword of Gideon" may have contributed a motif to further biblical legends. In Josh. 5:13–15, a man appeared before Joshua with a drawn sword in hand. He claimed himself to be the "commander of the army of Yahveh" and Joshua accepted him as such. The tale concludes with an allusion to the call of Moses (Exod. 3:5). In Num. 22:22b–35, an angel of Yahveh took his stand in the road, with a drawn sword in hand, and accomplished the conversion of Balaam to the religion of Yahveh.

Like the legends of Moses and Joshua, the origin legend of the Abiezerite oracle at Ophrah descends from the premonarchic era when psychoactive substances were publicly known and respected. Matters that premonarchic tradition treated openly later became secrets, due presumably to a lapse of popular interest in psychedelic substances, together with the rise of alternative prophetic practices that were based on hypnosis and sensory deprivation.[32]

Even the earliest texts maintain a certain degree of pretense concerning psychoactive substances; but I hesitate to consider them esoteric. The transparency of the deceptions indicates the sort of open secret, widely attested anthropologically, that is shared by many societies' adults but not by their young children. Just as our own little ones are taught, both orally and through literature, television, and films, to believe that Santa Claus and the Tooth Fairy bring them gifts, so ancient oral traditions that were always addressed simultaneously to children and adults asserted that manna ("What is it?") was eaten in the wilderness. The transparent riddle was presumably intended to avoid encouraging children to experiment with ergot on their own. Through a failure in educating adults, the deception later extended to them as well. What had anciently been intended as metaphors and symbolic allusions were unwittingly reified as miraculous violations of nature.

The early legends exhibit neither polemic nor apologetic. Their accounts of cultic practices make simple and unembarrassed affirmations. An apologetic tone may be detected, however, in the legend of the threshing floor of Araunah. Here, on the site where Solomon's temple was built, a national tragedy coincided with an ecstatic vision. In the days of the wheat harvest, a plague killed seventy-seven thousand men (2 Sam. 24:15). As the plague approached Jerusalem, David saw the destroying angel by the threshing floor of Araunah the Jebusite and he prayed to Yahveh (verses 16 and 17). Yahveh commanded the destroying angel to desist; and the prophet Gad, whose name means "coriander"—the flavor of manna (Exod. 16:31)—instructed David to raise an altar to Yahveh on the threshing floor (verses 16b, 18).

It is implicit that the plague (verse 15) was an infestation of the wheat harvest (verse 15). It is explicit that David, like Gideon, beheld an angel by a threshing floor and consequently founded a priestly establishment on the holy site (verses 17 and 18).

Polemic about the Manna Tradition

The development of the manna tradition between the premonarchic period and the era of the Priestly writer involved the passage of a psychedelic sacrament from public knowledge to esoteric priestly lore. A corresponding change occurred in the cult, where the bread of the Presence ceased to be available for public consumption and became an exclusively priestly privilege. The historical development may be explained, in part, as a response to polemics that were mounted against it.

The most vehement polemic extant is the complaint about manna in Num. 11:1–9. Also deriving from the Elohist (E) source document is a narrative account of the draught ordeal. In E's polemic against the golden calf, Moses determined the identities of the sinners through the juridical procedure.[33] "And he took the calf which they had made, and burnt it with fire, and ground it to powder, and scattered it upon the water, and made the people of Israel drink. . . . Yahveh sent a plague upon the people, because they made the calf which Aaron made" (Exod. 32:20, 35).

E portrayed Moses treating the golden calf as though it were the toxic ingredient of a draught ordeal. The polemic was addressed against the bovine statuary that Jeroboam installed at the cult centers of Bethel and Dan (1 Kings 12:28–30). The motif served simultaneously to condemn the use of ergot as a component within the cult of the golden calf. Ergot was apparently used by the Aaronid priests of Bethel as well as by the Aaronid priests of Jerusalem. The Levites' use of swords to kill the calf worshipers (Exod. 32:27) may be treated as further criticism of ergot. The motif implies that the draught ordeal was inadequate; the plague that it induced did not adequately punish the guilty.

The source document that is known as the Ark narrative[34] clarifies what was at stake from the standpoint of the Jerusalem priesthood. The narrative engages in polemic against the Elid priests of Shiloh (1 Sam. 2:12–17, 22–25; 4:1b–21) while praising the Ark itself (1 Sam. 5–6). The coincidence of polemic and apologetic suggests that the Ark narrative was originally composed in defense of Solomon's policies. Solomon both expelled the Elids from Jerusalem (1 Kings 2:26–27) and built a temple in which he installed their ark (1 Kings 8).

Solomonic propaganda may have been furthered by the Ark narrative's assertions that the Ark caused deaths when it was in Elid keeping. The circumstances of the deaths are notable. When the Philistines returned the Ark to Israel, it was harvesttime, and the deaths occurred in a field where wheat was being harvested

(1 Sam. 6:13–14,19). The other occasion when the ark of the covenant caused death similarly involved grain. When David attempted to fetch the Ark to Jerusalem, tragedy struck on the threshing floor of Nacon, when Uzzah touched the Ark and died (II Sam. 6:6-7). Both tales of fatality can be understood in the context of the draught ordeal and/or death-revival experiences. The sons of Eli were guilty, the narrative states, of abusing their priestly office for both fraudulent economic gain and illicit sexual relations with women. They deserved the deaths that they met.

E's polemic was directed against Aaronid priests, primarily at Bethel but also implicitly in Jerusalem. The polemic of the Ark narrative, which stemmed from Aaronids in Jerusalem, defended their expropriation of the Ark that the Gibeonite priests of the Elid dynasty had controlled in the premonarchic era. The Ark narrative's polemic was directed against a priesthood whose many sinful activities had ostensibly caused their ritual use of ergot to be deadly. Polemic was not directed against a pious use of the same psychedelic sacrament in the Sabbath-day offerings of the bread of the Presence.

The Aaronid response to E's polemic was presented in P's version of the story of Moses striking the rock at Kadesh. Referring not to the historical Moses, but to the lineage of priests who claimed descent from Moses and wrote the E text, P asserted that Moses' action at Kadesh had been a sin for which Moses had been denied entrance into the Promised Land.

> And Yahveh spoke to Moses, saying, "Take the rod, and assemble the congregation, you and Aaron your brother, and tell the rock before their eyes that it give its water; so you shall bring water out of the rock for them. . . ."
> And Moses lifted up his hand and hit the rock with his rod twice; and much water came out, and the congregation drank, and their animals. But Yahveh said to Moses and Aaron, "Because you did not trust in me, to sanctify me before the eyes of the children of Israel, therefore you shall not bring this assembly into the land that I have given them. (Num. 20:7-8, 11–12)

Writing at Hezekiah's court, in the years immediately after the destruction of the northern kingdom of Israel, P was offering a theological interpretation of the kingdom's demise. For P, E's motif of striking the rock while maintaining verbal silence was an alternative to speaking publicly in order to produce the miraculous water. P presented Moses' failure to enter the Promised Land as a consequence of secrecy about manna. Moses exhibited a lack of trust in Yahveh, and, by failing to discuss his sacrament openly, failed to sanctify Him publicly.

Prophetic Initiations

I have argued that a psychedelic substance was administered by Moses to the Israelites during the historical event that was remembered in legend as the miraculous provision of both manna and water in the wilderness. The psychedelic substance was subsequently ingested by priestly diviners of the premonarchic Gibeonite-Josephite tradition. The legend of Gideon suggests that his initiation, which was unequivocally ecstatic, involved the use of a psychoactive substance; but there is no indication that any of Gideon's subsequent activities as a diviner involved ecstasies of any kind.[35] The Elid priests are similarly known to us primarily as diviners. In the early Israelite period, late in the eleventh century B.C.E., both David and his men were eligible to partake of the Elid showbread at Nob; and the Yahwist (J) source reflects the standards of David's time and power base in Judah. Aaronid use of the sacrament at Bethel was condemned in the Elohist source, possibly late in the tenth century;[36] but the sacrament's use persisted in the north in the ninth century among the prophets Elijah and Elisha. In the late eighth century, manna was for the first time explicitly portrayed as a psychedelic substance, possibly in connection with the ecumenical purposes of Hezekiah's revival of the Passover festival (2 Chron. 30); but the Priestly writer nevertheless reserved the use of manna to priests and Levites.

Use of the psychedelic sacrament in an initiatory context is also indicated in the cases of Jeremiah and Ezekiel, for both of whom ecstasies were lifelong practices. The powerful prophet of the last days of Solomon's temple and his younger contemporary, the first great prophet of the Babylonian captivity, differed emphatically in many respects; but both cultic prophets apparently came by their vocations through initiations into the priestly esoterica of the manna tradition.

Jeremiah's book commences with an account of his divine call to become a prophet. We may note selected images.

> Then Yahveh put forth his hand and touched my mouth; and Yahveh said to me,
>
>> "Behold, I have put my words in your mouth.
>> See, I have set you this day
>> over nations and over kingdoms,
>> to pluck up and to break down,
>> to destroy and to overthrow,
>> to build and to plant."
>
> And the word of Yahveh came to me, saying, "Jeremiah, what do you see?" And I said, "I see a stick of almond." Then Yahveh said to me, "You have seen well, for I am watching over my word to perform it." (Jer. 1:9–12)

Jeremiah's sight of an almond stick—*maqel*, "stick"; "cane," "cudgel", not *'es*, "tree"; "wood"; "(unhewn) stick," as in Exod. 15:25 and 1 Kings 17:12—alluded to the legend of Aaron's rod: "and behold, the rod of Aaron for the house of Levi had sprouted and put forth buds, and produced blossoms, and it bore ripe almonds" (Num. 17:23). In legend, Aaron's rod was placed before the ark of the covenant (Num. 17:25), which was historically kept in the holy place in the Jerusalem temple. The origin legend of Aaron's rod presumably pertained to an object that Jeremiah was shown during his initiation as a cultic prophet. The identity of the object is indicated by its legendary function. In P, Moses employed Aaron's rod to produce water from the rock at Meribah (Num. 20:8, 11). The motif was an integral component of the manna tradition.

Jeremiah referred briefly to his call in the middle of a later prophecy.

Your words were found,
and I ate them;
and your word became for me a joy
and the delight of my heart;
and I was called by your name:
Yahveh of hosts. (Jer. 15:16)

The Yahveh who touched Jeremiah's mouth at his initiation (1:9) was presumably also a priest who acted in a ritual capacity on behalf of Yahveh.[37] The touch that Jeremiah felt on his mouth (1:9) and his experience of eating the words of Yahveh (15:16) may be taken at face value, as references to his ingestion of an edible substance. Because eating the substance gave Jeremiah access to Yahveh's words, the sacrament must have been psychoactive. If the substance was prepared in water, the role of Aaron's rod in the initiatory procedure may be explained.

Similar motifs occur in Ezekiel's account of the vision during which he received his prophetic mission.

And I saw, behold! a hand was sent toward me. And behold! in it was the scroll of a book. He spread it before me. It was written on the front and on the back. There was written on it lamentation, and mourning, and woe. He said to me, "Son of man, what you have found, eat. Eat this scroll. And go, speak to the house of Israel." So I opened my mouth and he fed me this scroll. Then he said to me, "Son of man, your stomach will eat and your guts will fill with this scroll that I give you." So I ate it. In my mouth it was as sweet as honey. (Ezek. 2:9–3:3)

Because this passage occurs at the end of Ezekiel's inaugural vision, the vision must itself have been induced by other means. In his vision, Ezekiel was told to accept an invitation to be initiated into the manna, and he envisioned himself doing so. The wordplay in verse 10a indicates that Ezekiel's narrative had an esoteric significance. The verb *yifrosh* means both that "he spread" and that "he gave an exegesis" of the scroll. The description of the scroll as being written on two sides (verse 10b) is inconsistent with literary practice in Ezekiel's era. Parchment scrolls were not written on both sides until the beginning of the common era, when the technology of tanning improved markedly.[38] Ezekiel's allusion is unmistakably to the stone tablets of Moses, which were similarly written on two sides (Exod. 32:15). Ezekiel's image also implied that his literary practice of double levels of meaning was deliberate. Finally, in remarking that "lamentation, and mourning, and woe" (Ezek. 2:10c) tasted "as sweet as honey" (3:3c), Ezekiel acknowledged the dangers of manna, even as he boasted of its sweetness.

Epilogue

The earliest tradition of the manna that has come down to us requires us, in God's name, to preserve, make public, and honor the psychedelic sacrament.

> And Moses said, "This is what Yahveh commanded: Let an omer of it be kept throughout your generations that they may see the bread with which I fed you in the wilderness, when I brought you out of the land of Egypt." And Moses said to Aaron, "Take a jar, and put an omer of manna in it, and place it before Yahveh, to be kept throughout your generations. (Exod. 16:32–33)

These are the words of the Yahwist and Priestly writers, writing at the courts of King David and King Hezekiah in the tenth and eighth centuries B.C.E. They are the official teachings of Solomon's temple.

The available evidence suggests that manna was used sacramentally in ancient Israel in a straightforward manner. One ate the showbread and awaited the occurrence of a psychedelic experience. On the occasion of one's first experience, the person who supplied the showbread enacted the role of Yahveh and, once the psychedelic experience was underway, pronounced the name of Yahveh. In this manner, the experience was guided in a religious direction.

Making a ritual of the celebration was presumably an option that was intended to be helpful for novices. An inquiring attitude was apparently all that is necessary. Yahveh told Jeremiah: "Call to Me, and I shall answer you, and tell you great tidings, and obscurities that you did not know" (Jer. 33:2).

TWO

Knowledge of Good and Evil

$\mathcal{T}$he Hebrew Bible's teachings concerning the interpretation of prophetic experiences were intended to apply, in my opinion, to alternate states that were induced not only through the sacramental use of psychedelic drugs, but also through sensory deprivation and/or mental imaging (visualization).[1] The doctrines are not specific to psychedelic states and cannot be used to demonstrate that psychedelic sacraments were in use. The one notable exception to this general rule is the riddle of the trees in Eden.

The Hebrew Bible records that when Nathan prophesied Yahveh's everlasting covenant with David's lineage, David entered the holy of holies in order to pray. In the course of his meditations (2 Sam. 7:18–29), David referred to Nathan's prophecy with wonderment, saying, "And this the *torah* of Adam!" (verse 19). The phrase has puzzled commentators for centuries. In my view, the biblical text had David allude to an interpretation of the tale of Adam and the trees of Eden that was current in David's time. Because the word *torah* literally meant "instruction" and in idiomatic usage meant either "oracle" or "doctrine," "law," David's remark may be taken in either of two ways. The text may have intended David to say that the prophecy of Yahveh's covenant with the House of David was either an oracle of Adam, that is, a prophecy of the same type as Adam's revelations, or it may be taken to mean that the dynastic prophecy was in conformance

27

with a doctrine or law of Adam. Whichever nuance is preferred, the text had David express wonderment that the revelation of the Davidic covenant was a true prophecy and not a false one. The touchstone of true prophecy was the example of Adam.

How did David understand the story of Adam? According to the court historian who penned the history of the Absalom war and the succession of Solomon, a wisewoman of Tekoa, who had been prompted by the prophet Nathan, addressed David with the following words: "For my lord the king is like the angel of God to discern good and evil. . . . But my lord has wisdom like the wisdom of the angel of God to know all things that are on the earth" (2 Sam. 14:17b, 20b). The capacity "to discern good and evil" was consistent with the capacity "to know all things that are on the earth." Both wisdoms were angelic.

These were not vain words of flattery, spoken by chance and recorded by chance. They were deliberate statements by an author who was one of David's intimates. The statements disclose the personal religiosity of King David. Solomon's personal religiosity was described in very similar terms. When Yahveh appeared to Solomon in a dream at the sanctuary of Gibeon, he offered to grant the king a request. Solomon replied: "Give your servant therefore an understanding mind to govern your people, that I may discern between good and evil; for who is able to govern this your great people?" (1 Kings 3:9). The text had Yahveh employ a slightly different formulation in his pledge to fulfill Solomon's request: "You have asked for yourself understanding to discern what is right. . . . I will give you a wise and discerning mind" (1 Kings 3:11b, 12b). As the sequel proves, the capacity to discern between good and evil was understood to imply wisdom quite generally (1 Kings 4:29–34).

Traditional Jewish and Christian exegeses notwithstanding, the tale of the Garden of Eden (Gen. 3) should not be divorced from these explicit references to the personal piety of David and Solomon. The tale of "the tree of the knowledge of good and evil" concerns the same power that the two kings enjoyed "to discern good and evil." Like David and Solomon, Adam acquired powers of discernment that were angelic. The biblical narrator had Yahveh say so explicitly toward the end of the tale: "Behold, the man has become like one of us, knowing good and evil" (Gen. 3:22). The "us" to whom Yahveh referred were his heavenly courtiers, the angels.

A different expression of the same religious orientation was employed by the prophet Isaiah. Writing of the restoration of peace through a future Son of David, Isaiah prophesied: "The nursling child shall play over the hole of the asp, / and the weaned child shall put its hand / on the adder's den" (Isa. 11:8). The serpentine symbolism signified that the future Son of David, no differently than the historical David and Solomon, would possess the knowledge of good and evil. The symbolism of the snake was very possibly borrowed from the religious complex surrounding the goddess Asherah, who is best known as the great mother goddess of the Canaanite religion. The consort of the high god El, she was depicted as a nude woman, standing on a lion, holding one or more serpents in her hands. Her epithets included "She who treads on the sea," "the Lady of the Lion," and "the Lady of the Serpent."[2] In the northern kingdom of Israel, Asherah was an integral part of the religion of Yahveh. In both Israel and Judah, the Canaanite high god El was syncretized with Yahveh, and Asherah was regarded as Yahveh's consort, at least in some northern circles. Josiah's reform abolished her cult in the late seventh century B.C.E.[3] With the exception of the sacred trees and poles that were her cult objects,[4] biblical references to Asherah were largely suppressed. Israelite sculptures depicting mother goddesses, however, sometimes in conjunction with serpents, are common archaeological finds and attest to her historical popularity.[5]

Importantly, a further Canaanite epithet of Asherah was "the Living One," whose Hebrew form *havvah* is the name that is anglicized as "Eve."[6] Not a goddess but a legendary woman, Eve represents a slightly different accommodation of Canaanite Asherah in the southern kingdom of Judah. Eve was not in conflict with biblical monotheism because Judan religious authorities had euphemerized the goddess, converting her into a legendary human being. Once Eve was denied the status of a deity, she was permitted to remain closely associated with a snake and with sacred trees. The meaning of Eve's symbolism was still comprehensible and doctrinally acceptable in the late eighth century when Isaiah wrote. The meaning of Eve was suppressed a century later, however, as part of Josiah's suppression of her divine prototype, Asherah.

To interpret the original meaning of the tale of Eden, I would emphasize several observations that the historian of religions Mircea Eliade made about the many myths, belonging to different cultures, that tell of a fall from a primordial paradise. Myths of a primordial fall typically portray an initial period when all humanity enjoyed exceptional circumstances: "immortality, spontaneity, liberty, the ability to ascend to Heaven and 'easy access' to the gods, friendship with the animals and knowledge of their language."[7] The many variants that refer "to an actual means of communication between Heaven and Earth" maintain that it was easy to reach Heaven "by means of a tree, a vine, or a ladder, or by climbing a mountain."[8] The fall resulted from a ritual sin or another mythical event and accomplished the cessation of the paradisiacal state for humankind as a whole.

So much for the stories. When we instead examine the symbolism and ideas of paradise that are found in living religious practices, as distinct from mythology, we find that the circumstances that myths describe are not events of the fabulous past. Rather, the circumstances that all humanity enjoyed prior to the fall continue to be enjoyed during ecstatic religious experiences. Ecstatic experiences are thus "equivalent to a *return to the beginning*, a reversion to the mythical days of a 'Lost Paradise.'"[9] The myth and its cultic symbolism constitute, as it were, a "theory" of communication between humankind and the divine. The ecstatic, who alone has an *experience* in conformance with the mythic scenario, appreciates the myth as the "ideological infrastructure" of ecstasy.[10]

For the rest of the community, the myth may be less a theory of ecstasy than a belief concerning concrete events of the paradisiacal past. Because the differences in their points of view, the paradisiacal era may have different meanings for ecstatics and for the rest of their communities.[11] For ecstatics, the time of paradise is the living ecstatic moment. For others, paradise may be no more than the dead and distant past. It may instead, or additionally, be deferred to the future postmortem.

Because both David and Solomon were said to have possessed the angelic power to discern good and evil, we are obliged to interpret the tale of Eden as a theoretic explanation of the Kings' religious experiences. Let us examine the tale using this assumption. To begin, we may note that Adam was formed of the dust of the ground (Gen. 2:7) before Yahveh planted a garden in Eden, in the east (2:8a). Adam was placed in the garden only subsequently (2:8b). For the same reason, Adam's expulsion from the garden relocated him where he could "till the ground from which he was taken" (3:23). He was not created in the garden. He was taken from soil outside it. He did not commence in paradise and fall from it. Adam both entered the garden and left it. He commenced on earth, visited paradise, and returned to his earthly home—all during the course of his mortal life.

Ambiguity surrounds the trees of Eden, double entendre attends their introduction. We may understand the following words at face value: "Every tree that is pleasant to the sight and good for food, the tree of life in the center of the garden, and the tree of the knowledge of good and evil" (2:9). The Hebrew words *nekhmad lemareh*, "pleasant to the sight," can however, also carry the literal meaning, "desirable for a vision." Taken in the latter sense, we might punctuate the verse with a colon, rather than a comma, in order to bring out the poetic parallelism.

"Every tree that is desirable for a vision and good for food: the tree of life in the center of the garden, and the tree of the knowledge of good and evil."

Parallelism is a frequent aesthetic device in biblical verse.[12] In

some cases, two different things were brought into parallel relation; but in others, both parallel lines referred to the same thing.
Gen. 2:9 can be read either way. We may interpret the text to
mean that the tree of life, a cosmic axis in the center of the garden,
was "desirable for a vision," while the tree of the knowledge of
good and evil was "good to eat." An alternative reading, however,
is also possible. Let us explore it.

If *ex hypothesi* we have here an instance of parallelism where
the same thing is said in two different ways, only a single plant
was being discussed. The tree of life *was* the tree of knowledge.
An immediate advantage of this reading of the text is its ability
to resolve several textual difficulties. Yahveh commanded Adam,
"You may freely eat of every tree of the garden; but of the tree of
the knowledge of good and evil you shall not eat, for on the day
that you eat of it you shall die" (2:16–17). This verse is the basis
of the common rabbinic and Christian interpretation that the
tree of knowledge was a forbidden fruit. When the serpent asked
the woman whether any tree had been forbidden, however, she
replied that "God said, 'You shall not eat of the fruit of the tree
which is in the center of the garden, neither shall you touch it, lest
you die'" (3:3). Here it the tree of life, the tree in the center of the
garden, that was forbidden. Are we to understand that Eve was
confused and mistaken?

Apparently not. The serpent replied to the woman by discussing the tree that conferred divine knowledge of good and evil. It
said: "You will not die; for God knows that when you eat of it your
eyes will be opened, and you will be like gods, knowing good and
evil" (3:4–5). The serpent referred clearly to the tree of knowledge. If Eve had been confused, she was confused no longer. The
woman's subsequent actions pertained, however, to a single tree
that was described simultaneously as edible, a delight to the eyes,
and a source of wisdom: "When the woman saw that the tree was
good for food, and that it was a delight to the eyes, and that the
tree was to be desired to make one wise, she took of its fruit and
ate" (3:6). "A delight for the eyes" is not the same Hebrew

phrasing as "desirable for a vision" in Gen. 2:9. But the Hebrew wording is another way of expressing the same double entendre: good to look at, and good for visions. The phrase alluded to the tree of life, while the reference to "a source of wisdom" alluded equally clearly to the knowledge of good and evil.

Because the text twice identifies the forbidden tree as the tree of knowledge, once as the tree of life, and once as both trees simultaneously, it is significant that the final references indicate that only a single tree was forbidden. When Yahveh accused Adam of violating his commandment, he referred unmistakably to a single tree: "Have you eaten of the tree of which I commanded you not to eat?" (3:11). Yahveh's curse upon Adam similarly specified a single but unidentified tree: "you have eaten of the tree of which I commanded you, 'You shall not eat of it'" (3:17).

To make sense of the tale, I suggest that only a single tree has been in question throughout. The different verses vary as to whether they refer to the tree of life, the tree in the center, the tree that is good to see (or good for visions), or the tree of knowledge of good and evil. But the logic of the narrative requires us to understand that however it may be named, the fruit of a tree that was prohibited was later eaten. Traditional Jewish and Christian readings ignore the references to the tree of life, the tree in the center, and the tree good to see. They interpret the tree as the tree of knowledge throughout. I suggest, however, that we do not need to ignore any of the text. We need only to interpret all of the epithets as references to a single tree.

Another puzzle of the tale of Eden is that the serpent was right in describing the fruit of the tree as edible. It was not poisonous. Neither the woman nor Adam died from eating it. Adam was instead told: "You shall return to the ground, for out of it you were taken; you are dust, and to dust you shall return" (3:19). This prophecy cannot be treated as a literal fulfillment of Yahveh's warning "on the day that you eat of it you shall die" (2:17). Adam did not die that day. On the day that he ate he was told that he would die at a future time.

Traditional Jewish and Christian interpretations of Yahveh's prophecy of Adam's future death are equally problematic. When the creation of human mortality is treated as a metaphoric fulfillment of Yahveh's warning of Adam's immediate death, it stretches the plain sense of the text beyond recognition. It also transforms Yahveh's friendly warning about a dangerous plant into a cruel and vindictive threat to cause human hardship. Moreover, the biblical text plainly intended Yahveh's initial warning to presuppose that Adam was mortal. Adam had been taken from the dust of the ground and had never been other than mortal. A plant could cause his death only because he was mortal.

Our obligation is to understand the text in a way that does not render it meaningless. Yahveh's prophecy of human mortality must be interpreted as having reminded Adam of the already existing fact of his mortality. Yahveh revealed nothing to Adam that he did not already know. The revelation presumably frightened Adam very badly. It was an instance, I suggest, of an experience of ecstatic death: an acute anxiety attack that manifests as a vision of immediately impending death.

When Yahveh's warning about Adam's immediate death is interpreted as a reference to an experience of ecstatic death, rather than to his bodily demise, the narrative falls tidily into place. It concerns a psychedelic plant that is able to facilitate both the interior mental dialogue of prophecy and the experience of ecstatic death.

King David's "law of Adam" (2 Sam. 7:19) enters into the tale, I suggest, in its curious conclusion. Adam was expelled from the garden "lest he put forth his hand and take also of the tree of life, and eat, and live for ever" (Gen. 3:22). Adam's expulsion from the garden apparently removed the possibility that he would acquire an immortality that he had never as yet possessed. If *ex hypothesi* the tree of life and the tree of knowledge were both names for a single plant, the conclusion of the tale obliges us to understand that one tree had two aspects that could not be encountered simultaneously. If we understand the effects of eating of the tree not as concrete primordial realities but as living ecstatic experiences, there is no paradox. A single practice of ecstasy was presupposed, but the psychedelic experience might have variable outcomes. The plant might confer wisdom. It might instead confer immortality. When it provided knowledge, it was edible. The death that it caused was an ecstatic death, a revelation of the knowledge of mortality. What was forbidden was the tree's use to acquire immortal life. When the ecstasy seemed to provide the unattainable goal of joining the company of God and the angels, that is, of divinization and immortality, psychedelic experience was being interpreted in a doctrinally unacceptable manner. The tale of Eden acknowledged that the same plant that facilitated prophecy might also facilitate divinization; but the *torah* of Adam insisted on human mortality and the incomparability of God.

THREE

Philo of Alexandria

*P*hilo of Alexandria is believed to have lived from approximately 20 B.C.E. to 50 C.E. The one certain date in his life pertains to his participation, in his old age, in an unsuccessful Jewish embassy to Caligula in 43 C.E. Philo belonged to an aristocratic family of Alexandrian Jews and was extremely well learned in classical literature and philosophy of both classical (fifth and fourth centuries B.C.E.) and Hellenistic (imperial Greek and Roman) periods. His philosophical writings pioneered the reconciliation of the biblical and Greek philosophical traditions by wedding Jewish biblical exegesis to Middle Platonic philosophy.[1] To make his case, Philo frequently resorted to allegorical interpretations of Scripture. His Greek-language writings were seminal for the early Christian church, but they were not preserved by Jews.[2] Rabbinic Judaism may have been influenced, however, by Philo's introduction of allegorism; rabbinic tradition preserved the memory that Hillel the Elder, whose hermeneutical innovations transformed Pharisaism into rabbinism, was deeply versed in allegorism.[3] Hillel was an exact contemporary of Philo's.

In a major scholarly study, Erwin Ramsdell Goodenough argued that the writings of Philo attest to a Jewish mystery of which Philo was an initiate.[4] Widely celebrated in classical Greece and the Hellenistic world, the mysteries were secret rites or, in another sense of the term, the religious groups that held secret rites that consisted of ecstatic initiations.[5]

> The mysteries were . . . composed of individuals who decided, through personal choice, to be initiated into the profound realities of one deity or another. Unlike the official religions, in which a person was expected to show outward, public allegiance to the local gods of the polis or the state, the mysteries emphasized an inwardness and privacy of worship within closed groups. . . .
>
> The word *mystery* (*mysterion* in Greek) derives from the Greek verb *myein,* "to close," referring to the closing of the lips or the eyes. . . . an initiate, or *mystes* (plural, *mystai*) into the *mysterion* was required to keep his or her lips closed and not divulge the secret that was revealed at the private ceremony. Vows of silence were meant to ensure that the initiate would keep the holy secret from being revealed to outsiders.[6]

Philo referred repeatedly to divine or holy mysteries of the Bible whose secrecy was to be preserved by their initiates.[7] He claimed to have been "initiated under Moses the God-beloved into his greater mysteries, and he characterized Moses as "the keeper and guardian of the mysteries of the Existent One."[8] The initiatory process consisted of a personal experience of revelation concerning the nature of God, which God provided to his initiate.

> There is a mind more perfect and more thoroughly cleansed, which has undergone initiation into the great mysteries, a mind which gains its knowledge of the First Cause not from created things, as one may learn the substance from the shadow, but lifting its eyes above and beyond creation obtains a clear vision of the uncreated One, so as from Him to apprehend both Himself and His shadow.
>
> If, however, thou art worthily initiated, and canst be consecrated to God and in a certain sense become an animate shrine of the Father, (then) instead of having closed eyes, thou wilt see the First (Cause). . . . Then will appear to thee that manifest One, Who causes incorporeal rays to shine for thee, and grants visions of the unambiguous and indescribable things of nature and the abundant sources of other good things.[9]

Philo asserted that the initiatory revelations conferred wisdom that facilitated remorse and ethical reform. "When, like initiates in the mysteries they have taken their fill of the revelations, they reproach themselves greatly for their former neglect and feel that they have wasted their time and that their life while they lacked wisdom is not worth the living."[10]

Even as Philo boasted of the biblical mystery, he wrote contemptuously of the corresponding Greek practices.

> [Moses] banishes from the sacred legislation the lore of occult rites and mysteries and all such imposture and buffoonery. He would not have those who were bred in such a commonwealth as ours take part in mummeries and clinging on to mystic fables despise the truth and pursue things which have taken night and darkness for their province, discarding what is fit to bear the light of day. Let none, therefore, of the followers and disciples of Moses either confer or receive initiation to such rites.[11]

Philo objected to the Greek mysteries on the grounds that their myths were fallacious and their rites involved both deception and foolishness. The mystery of Moses, by contrast, was devout, ethical, and philosophical.

Responding to Goodenough's thesis, Arthur Darby Nock expressed what was to become the scholarly consensus. He acknowledged that Philo had described Judaism in terminology appropriate to a mystery, but he claimed that Goodenough had not succeeded in demonstrating that Philo possessed secret Jewish teachings.[12] Philo's use of mystery terminology has consequently been treated as metaphoric.

It is my contention, however, that Philo was privy to the biblical secret of manna.[13] In two passages, Philo expressly associated the biblical mystery with the unleavened bread of Passover.

> They, who became partakers in the lesser before the greater mysteries, judged wisely, as I think, for they "baked their dough which they brought out of Egypt into buried unleavened cakes" (Exod. xii. 39). . . . And the method by which they softened it and wrought it to something better was revealed to them by divine inspiration, and they did not utter it aloud, but treasured it in silence. Their hearts were not lifted up by the revelation; rather they were bowed in submission, and all proud thoughts were humbled.

Being admitted into the inmost mysteries, she [the soul] will learn not to blab or babble them thoughtlessly, but to store them up and guard them in secrecy and silence. For it is written "make buried cakes," because the sacred story that unveils to us the truth of the Uncreated and His potencies must be buried, since the knowledge of divine rites is a trust which not every comer can guard aright.[14]

In a third passage, where Philo discussed both the unleavened bread of Passover and the showbread of the Temple, he defended their virtue by equating them with manna.

Let no one, then, turn away from affliction such as this, or think that, when the table of joy and feasting is called the bread of affliction, harm and not benefit is meant. No, the soul that is admonished is fed by the lessons of instruction's doctrine.

So holy is this unleavened bake-meat, that the oracles ordain that twelve unleavened loaves, corresponding to the number of the tribes, be set forth on the golden table in the inmost shrine, and these are called the loaves of setting forth (Exod. xxv. 29). . . .

Who then is so impious as to suppose that God is an afflictor. . . ? For God is good and the cause of what is good. . . .

Let us not, then, be misled by the actual words, but look at the allegorical meaning that lies beneath them, and say that "afflicted" is equivalent to "disciplined and admonished and chastened," and that "subjected to famine" does not mean that He brought about a dearth of food and drink, but a dearth of pleasures and desires and fears and grief and wrong-doings. . . And this is confirmed by the words that follow, "He fed thee with the manna." He who provided the food that costs no toil or suffering, the food which without the cares and pains of men came not from the earth in the common way, but was sent, a wonder and a marvel from heaven for the benefit of those who should use it—can we rightly speak of Him as the author of famine and affliction? Should we not on the contrary call Him the author of thriving and prosperity and secure and ordered living? But the multitude, the common herd, who have never tasted of wisdom, the one true food of us all, think that those who feed on the divine words live in misery and suffering, and little know that their days are spent in continued well-being and gladness.[15]

Like all of Philo's references to manna, this passage leaves crucial things unsaid, making of them a mystery that is reserved as a secret. What was manna? How can one taste of wisdom? In what sense is wisdom the one true food of us all? How can one eat divine words? Philo said enough publicly, however, that fellow initiates would be able to infer his meaning. Sound historiographic method obliges us neither to scorn his statements because they are incomplete, nor to build our case on statements that he did not make. We must instead attend very closely to precisely what Philo wrote.

Philo's associations of manna, Passover *matzot*, and the bread of the Presence constitutes an esoteric interpretation of the biblical text. The Bible nowhere makes the associations. It has the unleavened bread of the Passover replace the manna of the wilderness (Josh. 5:11–12), and it associates neither with the priestly bread of the Presence.

Philo explained the bread of affliction as a source of discipline, admonition, and chastening. His reversion, in the final sentence of this passage, from past-tense references to the era of Moses to present-tense references to his own time, all but gave away the secret. Philo also used the present tense elsewhere in stating that "the heavenly food of the soul, wisdom, which Moses calls 'manna,' is distributed to all who will use it."[16]

Commenting on Deut. 32:13, "suck honey out of the rock, and oil out of the hard rock," Philo explained that manna was prepared in the form of cakes. "In another place he uses a synonym for this rock and calls it 'manna.' . . . Out of it are made two cakes, the one of honey, the other of oil."[17]

Philo explicitly associated manna with the experience of individual verbal revelations.

> "Behold I rain upon you bread out of heaven, and the people shall go out and they shall gather the day's portion for a day, that I may prove them whether they will walk by My law or not" (Exod. xvi. 4). You see that the soul is fed not with things of earth that decay, but with such words as God shall have poured like rain out of that lofty and pure region of life to which the prophet has given the title of "heaven."[18]

Commenting on the drinking water that Rebekah provided in Gen. 24:17, Philo took the occasion to discuss manna.

> Wherefore in another passage sacred Scripture (orders) the measuring of the spiritual food that came forth from the ether and heaven like a spring and was called "manna" by the Hebrews, that it might not be too much for anyone or too little. . . . And to kindle the spirit of uttered discourse with a more perfect nature, the Father did not leave any part empty but completely filled the vessel of spirit, knowing that it naturally does not seek drink from her who has it, but from the water jar, to teach us that it is not mortal man who pours out blessings but the grace of God, which is too high for man and of which he prays to be thought worthy to partake, and that He give him to drink that which He had earlier put into (the vessel).[19]

Here the water jar, which is a "vessel of spirit" comparable to manna, had the power through "the grace of God" "to kindle the spirit of uttered discourse" with the Word of God. In other words, drinking the water, like eating manna, was able to facilitate the occurrence of a prophetic dialogue with God.

Philo also associated manna with experiences of mystical union. Where the Bible derived the term *man,* "manna," from the word "what," Philo invested the term with philosophical significance. "Manna [is] the most generic of substances, for the manna is called 'somewhat,' and that suggests the *summum genus.*"[20] "Manna is the divine word, eldest of all existences, which bears the most comprehensive name of 'Somewhat.'"[21] Deut. 8:2 associated manna with the divine word; but there was no biblical precedent for Philo's assertion that manna was the primal substance, the first existent. Here he drew instead on the Platonic concept of All-Being. By saying that manna was the most generic of substances, Philo associated it with experiences of mystical union in which the self is found to be solitary, timeless, and infinite.[22]

Reflecting the varieties of religious ecstasy that psychedelics are able to facilitate,[23] Philo elsewhere explained that manna was both the One Word and the many discrete words of revelation. "Let God then proclaim to the soul, 'Not on bread only shall men live, but on every utterance that goeth forth through the mouth of God,' that is to say he shall be fed both by all the word and by a part of it; for the mouth is a symbol of utterance or speech, and the statement is a part of speech."[24]

Philo also associated manna with the experience of visions. He connected the consumption of manna with the name Israel, which he explained by reference to the practice of seeing God. Philo several times stated that the name Israel means "he who sees God."[25] The philology is incorrect; it is the biblical name Reuel that signifies "he who sees God." Of the Hebrew patriarch, Philo nevertheless stated: "when, now deemed capable of seeing God, he . . . received the new name of Israel."[26] Elsewhere Philo described the people of Israel as "souls whose vision has . . . schooled itself to behold the uncreated and divine, the primal good."[27] A single extant passage links these ideas with the ingestion of manna.

> It is only the man of worth who sees, and therefore they of old called prophets "seers" (1 Sam. ix. 9). He who advances "outside" is called not only the seer, but the seer of God, that is Israel.
>
> But the others even if they do ever open their eyes have bent them earthwards; they pursue the things of earth and their conversation is with the dwellers in Hades. The one extends his vision to the ether and the revolutions of the heaven; he has been trained also to look steadfastly for the manna, which is the word of God, the heavenly incorruptible food of the soul which delights in the vision. But the others see but the onions and the garlic, which give great pain and trouble to their eyes and make them close, or the ill-smelling things.[28]

Philo referred to contemplation and vision interchangeably. Like the Yahwist's tale of the trees of Eden, Philo included both abstract conceptual experiences and visions among the effects of manna. He advocated neither religious experience exclusively. Perhaps the earliest explicit advocate of a negative theology, Philo maintained that God is unknowable in Himself and may only be inferred from his works. His preferred mystical experience consisted of an interior dialogue, a conjunction with the divine word, that permitted a mystic to experience, with immediacy, the unknowability of the God who reveals His word.[29] Precisely because Philo stands in the lineage of Platonic philosophers whose mystical experiences prioritized abstract concepts, his willingness not only to dignify but to privilege visions is notable. Philo called Israel the "nation of vision" because he literally meant *visions*.

Elsewhere he wrote:

> Why then need you still wonder that God showers virtue without toil or trouble, needing no controlling hand but perfect and complete from the very first? And if you would have further testimony of this can you find any more trustworthy than Moses, who says that while other men receive their food from earth, the nation of vision alone has it from heaven? The earthly food is produced with the co-operation of husbandmen, but the heavenly is sent like the snow by God the solely self-acting, with none to share his work. And indeed it says "Behold I rain upon you bread from heaven" (Exod. xvi. 4). Of what food can he rightly say that it is rained from heaven, save of heavenly wisdom which is sent from above on souls which yearn for virtue?[30]

Here the gift of manna is associated with the power of mystical vision and is discussed not as an ancient miracle but as an ongoing reality. This location of manna in the living present of Jewish experience quietly announced Philo's knowledge of a secret that was not generally known. The final question in this passage was equivocal. Noninitiates were to assume it rhetorical, an extravagant trope alluding to wisdom. Initiates were expected to treat it literally as a reference to an edible substance through which wisdom may be acquired—literally a *psychedelic*—"mind-expanding"—substance.

Only slightly less explicit than Philo's designation of manna as the "food of the soul which delights in the vision" was his phrasing in the following passage.

> Contact with knowledge without abiding in it is as if we should taste food or drink, and then be barred from receiving its nourishment to the full.
>
> . . . those who fed their soul with the heavenly food called manna. . . . ground and chafed it and made of it "buried" cakes

(Num. xi. 8), judging it right to crush and grind virtue's heaven-sent discourse, that its impress on their understanding might be the firmer.[31]

Having cited the Bible to establish that manna was something that was literally baked and eaten, Philo went on to allegorize the Bible's language, the firmer to impress its message on his readers.

Even Philo's allegorical interpretations sometimes alluded to the mystery of the psychedelic sacrament. Discussing the power of a vision of God to inhibit the passions, Philo abruptly and unnecessarily introduced the topic of manna.

> When he that sees God is studying flight from the passions, the waves become fixed as if frozen, that is to say the rush and growth and vainglory of the passions; "for the waves became solid in the midst of the sea" (Exod. xv. 8), in order that he that seeth Him that IS might pass beyond passion. The souls, therefore, that have indeed already had experience of the word, but are not able to answer the question, inquire one of another "What is it?" (Exod. xvi. 15). For it often happens that on finding a sweet taste in our mouths we are uncertain as to the flavour which has given rise to it, and that when we catch the scent of pleasant odours we do not know what they are. In the same way then the soul, when it has been gladdened, is often unable to say what the thing that gladdens it is. But it is taught by the hierophant and prophet Moses; he will tell it, This bread (Ibid.) is the food which God hath given to the soul, for it to feed on His own utterance and His own word; for this bread, which He hath given us to eat, is "this word."[32]

At one level, Philo was remarking that many initiates of the mystery were given a sweet taste to consume, but were not informed how the psychedelic edible was prepared. The plant responsible remained a secret that was reserved for their initiators. Philo simultaneously allegorized this level of meaning. He called manna "the food of the soul"[33] and explained that "the soul being a portion of an ethereal nature has . . . ethereal and divine food; for it is fed by knowledge in its various forms and not by meat and drink, of which the body stands in need."[34] The Bible's designation of manna as bread alluded to its preparation in an edible biscuit; but it also alluded to the power of psychedelic experiences, that is, of mind expansion or consciousness raising, to provide nourishment for the soul. Manna was both edible and psychoactive. Its psychoactivity nourished the mind, not the body.

A concern with the literal consumption of manna is similarly suggested by another passage where Philo abruptly reverted from a discussion of reason and wisdom, to emphasize the concrete sight, taste, and feeling of manna.

> When they sought what it is that nourished the soul (for, as Moses says, "they knew not what it was") (Exod. xvi. 15), they became learners and found it to be a saying of God, that is the Divine Word, from which all kinds of instruction and wisdom flow in perpetual stream. This is the heavenly nourishment, and it is indicated as such in the sacred records, when the First Cause in his own person says, "Lo, it is I that am raining upon you bread out of the heaven" (Ibid. 4); for in very deed God drops from above the ethereal wisdom upon minds which are by nature apt and take delight in Contemplation; and they see it and taste it and are filled with pleasure, being fully aware of what they feel, but wholly ignorant of the cause which produced the feeling. So they inquire "What is this" (Ibid. 15) which has a nature making it sweeter than honey and whiter than snow? And they will be taught by the seer that "This is the bread, which the Lord hath given them to eat" (Ibid. 15). Tell me, then, of what kind the bread is. "This saying," he says, "which the Lord ordained" (Ibid. 16). This Divine ordinance fills the soul that has vision alike with light and sweetness, flashing forth the radiancy of truth, and with the honied grace of persuasion imparting sweetness to those who hunger and thirst after nobility of character.[35]

Philo's concern was not to explain a difficult biblical passage by reducing the miracle of manna to an allegory about knowledge, but to cite divine reason and wisdom as advertisements for the mystery of manna.

Philo's use of mystery terminology was entirely appropriate. The mysteries originated when rites of ecstatic initiation were transformed from a secret practice of shamans, magicians, kings, priests, and warriors, into public religious devotions that were generally available to the adult populations of entire societies. The oldest demonstrable democratization of ecstatic initiations in the ancient world was the Israelite covenant under Moses. By comparison, the *telesterion* initiation hall at Eleusis was built in the classical period on the site of a templelike structure that dates only to the early sixth century B.C.E.[36] The initiation hall at Eleusis was built in the very years that Solomon's temple was destroyed. Philo had excellent reason, historical as well as phenomenological, to conceptualize the tradition of Moses as a mystery, even as he rejected the mysteries of the Greeks.

FOUR

Manna and the Eucharist

*I*n the canonical Gospels, when Jesus fed the five thousand with loaves and fishes (Matt. 14:15–21; Mark 6:35–44; Luke 9:12–17; John 6:1–15), early Christian storytelling devised a motif that alluded to the miracle of manna and quail in Moses' time. Like Moses, Jesus provided his followers with both bread and flesh. The story also echoed Elisha's miraculous feeding of one hundred men with twenty loaves of barley bread (2 Kings 4:42–44). These allusions to the Hebrew Bible were intended to indicate that Jesus stood in the tradition of Moses and Elisha–the tradition, as I have shown, of the mystery of manna. The gospel stories additionally included an original element. The motif of breaking the loaves prior to their distribution alluded to the sacramental breaking of the host during the Christian ritual of the Eucharist.[1]

It was no accident that the Christian Eucharist had the same basic features as the rite by which Jeremiah was initiated into prophesying. The main action of both rites was the administration and consumption of unleavened bread. In both rites, a priest performed the role of God. Jeremiah wrote that Yahveh had touched his mouth (Jer. 1:9), implying that a priest of Solomon's temple played Yahveh's role during the rite. Christian priests publicly enact the role of Jesus administering the host at the Last Supper. In both rites, those who ate the unleavened bread achieved union with God. Jeremiah stated that he was called by the name of Yahveh of hosts (Jer. 15:16). Christian communicants, according to Paul, experience Christ in themselves and themselves in Christ. Was Christianity heir to the manna tradition as it descended specifically from Jeremiah?

The equation of manna with the Christian Eucharist was complete. Matt. 15:32–39 and Mark 8:1–10 narrate a second feeding of four thousand people whom Matthew explicitly described as Gentiles (15:31). The term *eucharistesas,* "having given thanks" (Matt. 15:36; Mark 8:6), renders explicit the second feeding's association with the Eucharist. The second version presumably originated in oral tradition as a variant of the first.[2] Mark and Matthew preserved the duplication, whereas Luke did not, by having the second telling pertain to a feeding not of Jews but of Gentiles. The double narration of the story expanded the gospel teaching to reflect the evangelization of Gentiles and their admission to the Eucharist.[3]

"The four verbs 'take,' 'bless,' 'break,' and 'give' occur with minor variations not only in all six accounts of the two miraculous feedings and in that of the Emmaus meal [in Luke], but also in all four accounts of the Last Supper (including 1 Cor. 11:23–24)."[4] In this manner, the miracle of loaves and fishes, which alluded to manna and quails, was associated with the sacrament of communion in the very earliest strata of Christian tradition. Significantly, the breaking of the five loaves into enough pieces to feed five thousand people expressed, in a completely original way, the sufficiency of a minute quantity of heavenly bread.

It was only the author of John, however, who explicitly disclosed the narratives' concern with a psychoactive substance. John's version contains allusions to Moses' miracle of manna in Num. 11:13, 22, and to Elisha's miracle of the barley loaves in 2 Kings 4:42–44.[5] The term *eucharistein,* "thanksgiving," is used, and the narrative alludes to the ritual of the Eucharist.[6] In addition, John had Jesus state, "You are looking for me, not because you saw signs, but because you ate your fill of the loaves" (John 6:26). This saying, like so many of Jesus' discourses in the Johannine Gospel, was addressed to the gospel's readers by John, who wrote as a prophet in Christ's name. John did not intend the saying as a statement by the historical Jesus to a previous generation; rather, he intended the saying to be pertinent to his own contemporaries. You, the readers, John stated, see Jesus today because you eat the bread. People were able to seek Jesus visually because the loaves that they ate were psychoactive. Their ingestion made possible a vision of Jesus enthroned in glory. The statement's implicit concern with the early Christian practice of prophecy was made explicit a few verses later. When Jesus was explicitly questioned about manna, he replied in a discourse that was itself prophetic, claiming to be the bread of life (verses 31–35).

Spiritual Food

Like the gospel narratives of the loaves and fishes, Paul associated manna with the Eucharist. One of Paul's explicit references to manna may be interpreted as polemic against Jewish uses of ergot.

> I do not want you to be unaware, brothers and sisters, that our ancestors were all under the cloud, and all passed through the sea, and all were baptized into Moses in the cloud and in the sea, and all ate the same spiritual food, and all drank the same spiritual drink. For they drank from the spiritual rock that followed them, and the rock was Christ. Nevertheless, God was not pleased with most of them, and they were struck down in the wilderness. (1 Cor. 10:1–5)

In this passage, Paul compared the Israelites' passage through the Red Sea on dry land with the Christian sacrament of baptism. Manna and the water that Moses sweetened were compared with the bread and wine of the Eucharist.[7] The emphatic repetition of the word "all" stressed the unanimity of the Israelite experiences of God.[8] It was the heritage of "all" Israel that was being replicated or perpetuated in the Christian sacraments administered by Paul.

The description of manna as "spiritual food" and the water that flowed from "the spiritual rock" as "spiritual drink" have been variously interpreted by exegetes. The debate reflects differences in Protestant and Catholic interpretations of the Eucharist, which are projected onto Paul's account of the Israelites eating manna.[9] Commentators who, for reasons of anti-Semitism, insist that Paul was incapable of speaking well of Judaism reject the literal interpretation that the manna and water had spiritual effects on the Jews.[10] Käsemann rightly suggested that Paul's wording can only mean "food and drink which convey" spirit.[11] All that may legitimately be questioned is whether manna provided spirit in the form of a psychedelic experience or spirit was instead a euphemism for the theological significance of a sacramental rite. In my view, the Christian penchant for euphemisms arose historically as a consequence of the loss of the literal meaning of the New Testament documents. Paul should be taken at his word.

The author of Hebrews understood Paul as a fellow esotericist and took "spiritual food" to refer to a psychedelic substance. The assimilation of manna to the Eucharist was taken for granted when Heb. 6:4–6 spoke not of Israelites, but of Christians as "those who have once been enlightened, and have tasted the heavenly gift, and have shared in the Holy Spirit, and have tasted the goodness of the word of God and the powers of the age to come." A majority of the church fathers interpreted tasting the heavenly gift as a reference to the Eucharist.[12] Modern commentators, however, doubt the traditional interpretation and instead treat the clause as a metaphor that refers to spiritual gifts in general.[13] Once again, I advocate a literal reading of the text. The text openly refers to manna as being available for Christian consumption. What is more, manna was here explicitly psychedelic. Eating manna permitted a Christian to experience the Holy Spirit, to hear the word of divine prophecy, and to know, presumably through a vision, the angelic powers presently in New Jerusalem, who would become active on earth in the new age to come. These spiritual experiences are not predictable consequences of the public Eucharist, whether Catholic, Orthodox, or Protestant. The Letter to the Hebrews states that they are consequences of the manna, and there is no reason to doubt that they are such.

Interestingly, scholars are generally agreed that Paul, the author of Hebrews, and John the Evangelist either themselves knew the works of Philo, or depended on Hellenistic Jewish traditions to which Philo had been indebted.[14]

The Road to Emmaus

A further New Testament allusion to the psychoactivity of the Eucharist occurred in the tale, only transmitted by Luke, concerning an appearance by the resurrected Jesus on the road to Emmaus. Jesus accompanied two disciples on a walk from Jerusalem to the village of Emmaus but was unrecognized by his companions until he broke bread.[15] "When he was at the table with them, he took bread, blessed and broke it, and gave it to them. Then their eyes were opened, and they recognized him; and he vanished from their sight" (Luke 24:30–31). The blessing, breaking, and distribution of the bread were described in the same manner as in the gospel accounts of the loaves and fishes and the Last Supper.[16] Jesus' action differed from the Eucharist, however, in that he was already seated.[17] The bread on the road to Emmaus alluded to the public Eucharist but differed from it.[18]

What is implied by the disciples' initial failure to recognize their companion as Jesus, and their later capacity to do so, was their ability to see Jesus in his glory only after eating the broken bread. The phrase, "and their eyes were opened," was borrowed from Gen. 3:4, 7, where it was used to describe the consequences of eating of the tree of knowledge.[19] Jesus' sudden disappearance alluded to the angel who initiated Gideon at Ophrah of the Abiezerites.

The First Temptation

Matthew and Luke, borrowing *ex hypothesi* from a common source that scholars term *Quelle* (Q), meaning "source," detailed three temptations of Jesus in the wilderness. The first temptation employed motifs of the manna tradition.

> And the tempter came and said to him, "If you are the
> Son of God, command these stones to become loaves of
> bread."
> But he answered, "It is written,
> 'Man shall not live by bread alone,
> but by every word that proceeds from the mouth of God.'"
> (Matt. 4:3–4; cf. Luke 4:3–4)

On the surface, the tempter urged Jesus to speak words of magical command; and Jesus promptly matched the tempter's reference to bread with a biblical quotation. It is significant, however, that the tempter's remarks cited two traditional motifs of the manna tradition: bread and the rock out of which honey, oil, or water flowed. When the tempter suggested that Jesus produce bread by means of magic, he alluded to Moses' provision of manna in the desert.

Jesus immediately corrected the tempter's understanding of manna. He cited Deut. 8:3, which states: "He impoverished you, and made you hunger, and fed you the manna, which you did not know, nor did your ancestors know, in order to make you know that man does not live on bread alone, but man lives on all that comes from the mouth of Yahweh." By this statement, the Deuteronomic writer had asserted that manna was not merely a physically nourishing bread; it was more than bread alone. More clearly than Deuteronomy, however, Matthew credited manna with both nourishment and the prophetic word. Matthew mistranslated the Hebrew *kol*, "all" or "everything," as "every word."

Water into Wine

The Gospel of John stated that Jesus turned water into wine as "the first of his signs, in Cana of Galilee, and revealed his glory" (2:11). Miraculous transformations of water into wine were credited by the Greeks to Dionysus, the god of intoxication. The motif was replicated in ritual during the Dionysian feast at Andros, where fountains in the temple spouted wine instead of water.[20] The motif was also celebrated in myth. In *The Bacchae*, Euripides wrote:

> One woman
> struck her thyrsus against a rock and a fountain
> of cool water came bubbling up. Another drove
> her fennel in the ground, and where it struck the earth,
> at the touch of god, a spring of wine poured out.[21]

Working through two women he had possessed, Dionysus here matched and bettered Moses' miracle of drawing water from a rock. Dionysus' transformation of water into wine presumably referred to the practice in the Dionysian Mysteries of using henbane, mandrake, or another hallucinogenic plant of the nightshade family as an additive to wine.[22] The motif signified that the nightshade hallucinogens were equally effective when taken with water.

Philo, who presumably knew the Dionysian motif,[23] reworked it in a Jewish manner. Philo wrote: "But let Melchizedek instead of water offer wine, and give to souls strong drink, that they may be seized by a divine intoxication, more sober than sobriety itself."[24] Philo appropriated the allusion to a psychoactive sacrament, but he reworked the motif to refer to the psychedelic state of biblical prophecy, rather than the hallucinogenic state of Dionysus. Psychedelic states are technically pseudohallucinatory, not hallucinatory. One knows, while beholding a vision, that the vision is the content of one's imagination.[25]

John's gospel credited Jesus as having powers similar to those of Dionysus.[26] John's reference to Jesus as "the true vine" (15:1) implied that Dionysus was a false vine.[27] Whether John's reference to the manifestation of Jesus' glory belonged to an oral tradition used by the evangelist or was instead invented by the evangelist,[28] the text as we have it states explicitly that the wine had the function of revealing Jesus' glory. It was evidently psychedelic.

Not only was the term "glory" applied to a technical theological concept by several biblical writers, but the biblical theology was widely broadcast by Philo of Alexandria, a generation prior to Jesus' ministry. Philo wrote:

> What is the meaning of the words, "And the glory of God came down upon Mount Sinai" [Exod. 24:16]?
> . . . what is said to come down is clearly not the essence of

God, which is understood only as to its being, but His glory. And the notion of glory *(doxa)* is twofold. On the one hand, it denotes the existence of the powers, for the armed force of a kind is also called "glory." On the other hand, (it denotes) only a belief in and counting on the divine glory, so as to produce in the minds of those who happen to be there an appearance of the coming of God, Who was not there, as though He were coming for the firmest assurance of things about to be legislated.

What is the meaning of the words, "The form of the glory of the Lord (was) like a fire burning before the sons of the seeing one" [Ex 24:17]?

(This is said) because, as has been said before, the glory of God is the power through which He now appears; the form of this power is like a flame or rather, it is not but appears (to be so) to the spectators, for God showed not that which pertained to His essence but what He wished to seem to be to the amazement of the spectators. . . . there was an appearance of flame, not a veritable flame. . . . For they are silly and at the same time frivolous in belief who believe that the fire is the essence of God when (Scripture) clearly proclaims that it is the form of the glory and power of God which appears but not the truly existing One, and that the fire is not His power but only His glory and that in the opinion of the spectators it appeared to their eyes not to be what it was. . . . That is the literal meaning.[29]

References to divine glory in the New Testament were continuous with the theological tradition of the Hebrew Bible and Philo. According to Paul, the glory of Jesus was to be beheld in this life, following a visionary's ascent to heaven, where the glorified Jesus sat enthroned in paradise.[30] Modern commentators work with a different theology when they acknowledge that the disciples only enjoyed an anticipation, in this life, of a beatific vision of Jesus resurrected in glory.[31]

The intoxicating water that produced visions of the glory alluded, I suggest, to the water that Moses sweetened with a tree at Marah. The water was described in John as wine because the gospel writer wished to associate the psychedelic beverage with the sacramental wines of Dionysus and the Christian Eucharist. An allusion to the water's color is also possible. The Fourth Book of Ezra, a Jewish apocalypse that is dated to c. 90 C.E., speaks explicitly of the fiery color of a psychedelic water.

> And on the next day, behold, a voice called me, saying, "Ezra open your mouth and drink what I give you to drink." Then I opened my mouth, and behold, a full cup was offered to me; it was full of something like water, but its color was like fire. And I took it and drank; and when I had drunk it, my heart poured forth understanding, and wisdom increased in my breast, for my spirit retained its memory; and my mouth was opened, and was no longer closed. (4 Ezra 14:38–41)[32]

The color of the water may have alluded to the fiery appearance of the glory of God.

Whatever the reason for its color, the fiery appearance of the water in 4 Ezra also compares with the concept of Jesus' baptism with fire and the Holy Spirit in Matt. 3:11.[33] Fire was the color of the water whose consumption facilitated experience of the Holy Spirit.

The Hidden Manna

Most allusions to manna in the New Testament are equivocal. They can neither be proved nor disproved to have referred knowingly to ergot. If we read them from the perspective of an esoteric tradition on the psychoactivity of manna, they are comprehensible in that context; but there is no need to read them in such a manner. Consider, for example, the reference in Revelation to "the hidden manna" (Rev. 2:17). The unexplained and enigmatic phrase likely refers to the tradition, recorded in 2 Macc. 2:4–7, that Jeremiah rescued the jar of manna from Solomon's temple at the time of its destruction and hid it underground in Mount Nebo. Upon the coming of the Messiah, Jeremiah will return the Ark and its contents to a new temple in Jerusalem.[34] Alternatively, Rev. 2:17 may have alluded to a belief that a celestial treasury of manna would be opened in the end times.[35] The eschatological prediction is found, among other places, in 2 Bar.

29:8, a Jewish apocalypse written in the early second century C.E.: "and it will happen at that time that the treasury of manna will come down again from on high, and they will eat of it in those years because these are they who will have arrived at the consummation of time."[36] Although both Revelation and 2 Baruch imply that their authors believed the end-times to have arrived, neither states that the expected return of manna had already occurred.

Other New Testament passages are similarly equivocal. Many passages repeat motifs and themes from the manna stories of the Hebrew Bible without providing any indication that an esoteric significance is necessarily intended. In other cases, however, New Testament documents use traditional motifs in new ways, or introduce new motifs. When attempts to interpret esoteric subtexts lead to incoherence, as throughout Mark and Luke, with the single exception of the Emmaus pericope, it is appropriate to conclude that the authors were not aware of any esoteric significance in the motifs that they reworked. Conversely, when original materials are used in ways that permit coherent exegeses of esoteric subtexts, the possibility of chance remains, but the hypothesis of esoteric intentionality merits serious consideration. Several passages accordingly bear review.

The Gift That Moses Commanded

The tradition underlying the synoptic Gospels relate that Jesus healed a leper as his first public act of healing. The healing placed Jesus in the tradition of Moses and Elisha, who healed leprosy in the Hebrew Bible (Num. 12:10–15; 2 Kings 5:1–14). Because leprosy was considered curable in the statutes of Leviticus 13,[37] the biblical concept of leprosy evidently included skin ailments, such as elephantiasis, psoriasis, and vitiligo, in addition to Hansen's disease, or leprosy in the modern sense.[38]

After curing the leper, Jesus told the man, "See that you say nothing to any one; but go, show yourself to the priest, and offer the gift that Moses commanded, for a proof to the people" (Matt. 8:4; cf. Mark 1:44, Luke 5:12). The text has generally been explained by reference to Lev. 14:10, which requires that people offer animal and cereal sacrifices at the Jerusalem temple after their recovery from leprosy. The phrase "for a proof to the people," however, which appears in the synoptic Gospels, is not comprehensible in the context of the Levitical leprosy law. Modern exegetes have consequently resorted to euphemisms and metaphors in unsatisfactory efforts to make sense of the phrase.[39] I would prefer to interpret the gospel phrasing as an uncomplicated allusion to the literal text of Exod. 16:32, where Yahveh commands Moses to preserve an omer of manna "throughout your generations, that they may see the bread with which I fed you in the wilderness." The omer of manna was "a proof to the people."

The synoptic Gospel tradition asserted that Jesus asked the leper to carry a message to Jerusalem for him. In making his request, Jesus took for granted that the leper would go to Jerusalem in order to fulfill Lev. 14:10 by offering an animal sacrifice and being pronounced ritually clean. Jesus asked the man, since he was going to Jerusalem in any event, to explain to the priest how he had come to be healed of his leprosy. The man was to present the priest with a cereal offering that was psychedelic, as a means to announce Jesus' ministry to the Jerusalem priesthood.

Supporting this reading of the text, I note that the phrasing, "He stretched out his hand and touched him" (Matt. 8:3; Mark 1:41; Luke 5:13), alluded to Moses' characteristic action in handling his rod in order to work miracles (see Exod. 9:23; 10:13, 22; 13:21). The synoptic Gospel tradition did not concern Jesus accommodating the priests' interest in Mosaic law. It concerned Jesus acting on the precedent of Moses, citing Moses' authority, and implicitly using Moses' so-called rod to work a miracle of healing.

Were Jesus and his movement persecuted, among other reasons, because it was the secret of the Jerusalem temple's showbread that they attempted to make public?

Plucking Grain on the Sabbath

The synoptic Gospels also contain the tale of Jesus and his disciples plucking grain in the grain fields on the Sabbath.

> At that time Jesus went through the grain fields on the Sabbath; his disciples were hungry, and they began to pluck heads of grain and to eat. But when the Pharisees saw it, they said to him, "Look, your disciples are doing what is not lawful to do on the sabbath." He said to them, "Have you not read what David did when he and his companions were hungry? He entered the house of God and ate the bread of the Presence, which it was not lawful for him to eat nor for those who were with him, but only for the priests. Or have you not read in the law that on the sabbath the priests in the temple break the sabbath and yet are guiltless? I tell you, something greater than the temple is here. But if you had known what this means, 'I desire mercy and not sacrifice,' you would not have condemned the guiltless. For the Son of Man is lord of the sabbath." (Matt. 12:1–8; cf. Mark 2:23–28; Luke 6:1–5)

Commentators have frequently remarked that the internal logic of Jesus' argument is faulty.[40] How can a violation of the bread of the Presence by David justify a violation of the Sabbath by Jesus' disciples? Matthew was evidently sensitive to the difficulty with Jesus' reply. He added the argument, paralleled in neither Mark nor Luke, regarding the violation of the Sabbath by temple priests.

Another problem with the text is its final sentence. Mark 2:27–28 reads: "Then he said to them, 'The sabbath was made for humankind, and not humankind for the sabbath; so the Son of Man is lord even of the sabbath.'" This phrasing is paralleled by a rabbinic statement, "The sabbath is delivered unto you, you are not delivered to the sabbath."[41] Because the tradition underlying the synoptic Gospels seeks to defend the actions not of Jesus but of his disciples, it is likely that the tradition originally cited the rabbinic teaching concerning humanity in general, adding a conclusion, "for man is master of the sabbath." In the process of translation, the Aramaic *bar nesha*, literally, "son of man," but idiomatically, "man, human being," was taken to refer not to humanity in general, but specifically to Jesus as Son of Man.[42] In this manner, Jesus was said to have used the term *kyrios*, "lord," in a developed Christological sense appropriate to the early Church, but that was inconsistent with the historical Jesus' self-references.[43] Mark failed to appreciate these difficulties with the translation and so transmitted the error to posterity. Matthew, who possibly knew the rabbinic version of the saying, presumably recognized the difficulty with Mark. Because he accepted the received tradition of the saying's application to Jesus, Matthew eliminated the first half of the saying, with its explicit references to humanity in general.

Yet a further difficulty with the narrative is identifying the supposed violation of the Sabbath.[44] According to Deut. 23:25–26, a plant in another person's orchard or field may lawfully be picked for immediate consumption. For example, a fruit may be plucked from a tree if it is immediately eaten. Plucking grain can be construed as reaping, which is forbidden on the Sabbath,[45] only if the grain is cropped through the use of an implement or is transported away from the field before it is eaten. What exactly did Jesus' disciples do? The verbs in the different gospels vary. Mark has "making a way" and "plucking" and so is ambiguous as to whether work was being done on the Sabbath. Matthew, however, who knew Jewish ritual law, has "plucking" and "eating," and Luke followed Matthew with "plucking," "rubbing with the hands," and "eating." Both phrasings specify that consumption was immediate. The evangelists, who were here presumably dependant on Q, were explicit that Sabbath laws were *not* violated.

Moreover, because Jesus, in Matt. 12:3, replies to the Pharisees in a manner that ignores their concern with the Sabbath in verse 2, I suggest that at the time of the narratives's original composition, the Pharisees did not refer to the Sabbath. *Ex hypothesi* the tale underlying the synoptic Gospels originally had the Pharisees accuse, "Look, your disciples are doing what is not lawful to do." The qualifying phrase, "on the sabbath" (Matt. 12:2; Mark 2:24; Luke 6:2), would have been added by someone (possibly Mark[46]) who was unaware of the details of Jewish law and incorrectly supposed that the violation concerned work that was prohibited on the Sabbath.

The first four verses of the extant narrative can stand coherently on their own as the nucleus of the tale. When Jesus took his disciples into the grain field on the Sabbath, he defended his action by reference to David and the bread of the Presence. What was at stake in the narrative was not a violation of the Sabbath. What Jesus had to say in verses 3 and 4 pertained to the showbread. Alluding to 1 Sam. 21:1–6, Jesus cited the precedent of David who, with his men, entered the sanctuary at Nob and ate its showbread when he was fleeing King Saul. The text of Samuel has the priest Ahimelech state that the showbread could only be eaten "provided that the young men have kept themselves from women" (verse 4). David replies that not only have they kept away from women, but their eating utensils were "holy" (verse 5)— presumably ritually clean. To a modern historian, the exchange implies that in David's era, consumption of the showbread was available to the general public. It had not yet been restricted to the exclusive use of the priests (Lev. 24:9).

The tradition of the synoptic Gospels instead had Jesus acknowledge the Levitical usage that no one but priests might eat the showbread. The explanatory phrase, "which it was not lawful for him or his companions to eat, but only for the priests" (Matt. 12:4; Mark 2:26; Luke 6:4), however, cannot reasonably be attributed to the initial version of the narrative. Unlike Gentile Christian readers of the gospel, the Pharisees would not have needed the historical Jesus to explain the relation of David's action to the statute of Leviticus. The nucleus of the tale simply had Jesus' disciples eat grain, and Jesus defend their action by citing the precedent of David and his men eating the bread of the Presence. David's precedent provided license for those who were not priests to eat ergot, which they did on the Sabbath because Sabbath was the day on which priests ate the bread of the Presence.

Matthew plainly understood the narrative in this manner.

Alone among the gospels, Matthew had Jesus also say, "Or have you not read in the law that on the Sabbath the priests in the temple break the Sabbath and yet are guiltless" (Matt. 12:5). The citation from Hos. 6:6, preferring mercy to sacrifice, indicates that Matthew alluded to the work involved in the priestly practice of offering sacrifices on the Sabbath (Num. 28:9–10). Importantly, the Sabbath sacrifices included replacing the old showbread with freshly prepared cakes (Lev. 24:8).[47] In its Matthean context, the allusion to Sabbath sacrifices pointedly included the baking and transporting of the new showbread as permissible violations of the Sabbath. In this way, Matthew, who received the misinterpreted tradition that made reference to the Sabbath, contrived to insert an additional reference to the showbread, in order to restore the original concern of the tale.

Like the story of the message that Jesus sent with the leper to the temple, the gospel tale of Jesus educating his disciples in the botanical identification of the active ingredient of the showbread very possibly goes back to an eyewitness.

The Parable of Wheat and Tares

The parable of the wheat and tares, which is unique to Matthew's gospel, contains an element of polemic.

> Another parable he put before them, saying, "The kingdom of heaven may be compared to a man who sowed good seed in his field; but while men were sleeping, his enemy came and sowed weeds among the wheat, and went away. So when the plants came up and bore grain, then the weeds appeared also. And the servants of the householder came and said to him, 'Sir, did you not sow good seed in your field? How then has it weeds?' He said to them, 'An enemy has done this.' The servants said to him, 'Then do you want us to go and gather them?' But he said, 'No; lest in gathering the weeds you root up the wheat along with them. Let both grow together until the harvest; and at harvest time I will tell the reapers, Gather the weeds first and bind them in bundles to be burned, but gather the wheat into my barn.'" (Matt. 13:24–30)

Matthew had Jesus continue with the parables of the mustard seed and the yeast before he left the crowds and spoke privately with the disciples, giving them an interpretation of the parable of the wheat and tares (Matt. 13:36–43). The interpretation allegorizes the wheat as the children of the kingdom of heaven, the tares as sinners, and the harvest as the end times.

The narrative may simultaneously support an esoteric interpretation that alludes to the sacramental use of ergot. *Lolium temulentum*, "poisononous rye grass," "tares," "darnel," or "cockle," is a weed that infests grain crops. To sow darnel in a wheat field as an act of revenge was punishable under Roman law. Darnel's roots tangle with the roots of the grain, making it impossible to uproot a heavy infestation of the one without destroying the other.[48] In the present context, it is also significant that like cereal grasses, darnel may be infested by ergot.[49] If we assume that Matthew had an esoteric intention, we may conclude that by two sources of ergot he was contrasting two uses, one Christian and the other perhaps Jewish.

The Parable of Hidden Treasure

Immediately after Jesus explained the parable of the wheat and tares in private to his disciples, Matthew located the parable of the hidden treasure, "The kingdom of heaven is like treasure hidden in a field, which a man found and covered up; then in his joy he goes and sells all that he has and buys that field" (Matt. 13:44).

By having Jesus narrate the parable in private to his disciples, Matthew indicated that Jesus' interpretation of the wheat and tares was itself a parable that was in need of interpretation. Because the parable of hidden treasure directly follows the interpretation of the parable of wheat and tares, it implies that something more than wheat and tares was to be found in a grain field. In a grain field one might find the hidden treasure of the kingdom of heaven.

What Defiles a Person

Mark's tale of defilement had Jesus say, "There is nothing outside a man which by going into him can defile him; but the things which come out of a man are what defile him" (Mark 7:15). Matthew's phrasing referred specifically to the mouth: "It is not what goes into the mouth that defiles a person, but it is what comes out of the mouth that defiles" (Matt. 15:11). By referring to the mouth, Matthew's text alluded to Deut. 8:3, which states: "He impoverished you, and made you hunger, and fed you the manna, which you did not know, nor did your ancestors know, in order to make you know that man does not live on bread alone, but man lives on all that comes from the mouth of Yahweh."

Jesus' saying has traditionally been understood to refer to the needlessness of Jewish dietary observances *(kashrut)*.[50] Matthew, however, added a few verses that gave the saying a different meaning. "Then the disciples came and said to him, 'Do you know that the Pharisees were offended when they heard this saying?' He answered, 'Every plant which my heavenly Father has not planted will be rooted up. Let them alone; they are blind guides. And if a blind man leads a blind man, both will fall into a pit'" (Matt. 15:12–14).

Matthew diverted the significance of the pericope from the topic of *kashrut* when he introduced the concept of a plant. In rabbinic law, vegetables can themselves never be unkosher; they can become impermissible only through contact with unkosher foods, implements, or vessels. By having Pharisees object that Jesus defiled himself by eating a plant, Matthew introduced an idea that had nothing to do with *kashrut*. Anyone who knew Pharisaic practice, as Matthew and his original audience assuredly did, would have known that the controversy between Jesus and the Pharisees about eating a plant concerned something that was otherwise unknown—a secret or mystery. Moreover, because God may be said either to plant all plants, or to plant none, but cannot meaningfully be said to plant only some, the peculiarity of Matthew's turn of phrase draws attention to the mystery.

Importantly, the implication that the Pharisees were a plant that God did not plant is not conveyed by the sentence that speaks of the uprooting of the plant. The implication is instead conveyed by the juxtaposition of the further sentences that likened the Pharisees to blind guides. The separate origin of the two motifs is suggested by the difference between actively uprooting a plant and leaving a blind guide to come to grief on his own. The one saying urged Christians to oppose the Pharisees, the other to ignore them. Whether Matthew added the plant motif to a tradition that spoke of the Pharisees' blindness, or—less likely—vice versa, Matthew did not harmonize the two images. He instead permitted the motif of the plant to remain peculiar.

These several efforts by Matthew to provide clues regarding the botanical identity of the psychedelic sacrament tend to suggest that the mystery of manna was already becoming a lost knowledge among Christians by Matthew's time. Both the original tradition underlying the synoptic gospels and Q took for granted matters that Matthew felt called upon to explain.

Conclusion

The story of the loaves and fishes, which is shared by all four Gospels; Luke's narrative of Jesus' appearance on the road to Emmaus; John's tale of the water turned into wine; and Hebrews' rephrasing of an equivocal phrase in Paul refer explicitly to one or more psychedelic sacraments.

Precisely because they were misunderstood by Mark and Luke, the synoptic Gospels' references to the gift that Moses commanded and Jesus' reference to David eating the showbread indicate that the concern with a psychedelic substance, closely associated with grain, goes back to the earliest stratum of Christian tradition.

The first temptation of Jesus was told by Matthew and Luke, but not by Mark. Matthew alone narrated, and presumably composed, the parable of wheat and tares, the parable of hidden treasure, and the application to a plant of the synoptic Gospels' rejection of dietary restrictions.

To conclude, knowledge of the relation of manna, the priestly showbread, and psychedelic experiences induced through ergot was apparently transmitted by the historical Jesus to his disciples. The secret was known to the original storyteller whose work underlies the synoptic Gospels; to the storyteller whose work underlies the Q materials common to Matthew and Luke; to Matthew, John, and the author of Hebrews; and very probably also to both Paul and John of Patmos who wrote Revelation. Although Luke preserved the tale of Jesus' appearance on the road to Emmaus, neither Mark nor Luke appear to have been in the know.

In all likelihood, the traditional initiation of a prophet, as described by Jeremiah, was administered by the historical Jesus to one or more of his disciples. A public version of the initiation rite that substituted psychologically inactive substances for public use, was evidently instituted by the disciples after Jesus' crucifixion. Their institution of the Christian Eucharist served, among its other functions, to announce to all initiated Jews that Jesus' disciples practiced the traditional, secret, psychedelic initiations of the prophets of Israel.

FIVE

Rabbinic Midrash

*T*he Fourth Book of Ezra and the Second (Syriac) Book of Baruch, which mention a fiery, psychoactive water and the eschatological return of manna, respectively, are notable on several counts. They are the unique extant examples of Jewish apocalypses that attempted rapprochements with the rabbinacy. Their dates, c. 90 C.E. and shortly thereafter, respectively, suggest that they were efforts by apocalyptists to participate in the reorganization of Jewish religious life at Yavneh (Jamnia). Following the Judaeo-Roman War of 66–72 C.E., at least many of the quarreling sects of the Jews convened in the town of Yavneh under the leadership of the Pharisees, to pool their resources, work out their differences, and articulate a common form of Judaism that was agreeable to all.[1] After Yavneh, there were no longer any Pharisees or Sadducees. The term *rabbi*, "my master," which had earlier referred to school teachers, became the common term for a religious authority, and the rabbinacy was born.

Jewish apocalypses, as a genre, represent the major surviving literature of the Jewish mysticism of the period. The earliest examples were composed late in the third century B.C.E.; the last examples blended imperceptibly into the *merkavah*, "chariot," or *hekhalot*, "palace," mysticism of the rabbinic period. With the exception of 4 Ezra and 2 Baruch, the apocalypses were largely indifferent to the rabbinacy, either because they antedated its rise, or because they remained aloof from the rabbinic community.

Four Ezra shows the impact of the historical Jesus on Jewish apocalypticism. In Ezra's fourth vision, the heavenly city of Jerusalem descends onto the earth and the seer walks through the city, exploring its wonders (4 Ezra 10:27, 55–57). The vision deserves to be understood as an illustration of Jesus' distinctive teaching that the Kingdom of Heaven is available, in the present, to those who choose to enter it. The personality transformation that the seer undergoes in the course of the same vision[2] again attests to the influence of the early Christian message. The author of 4 Ezra nevertheless remained within Judaism, refusing to deify the historical Jesus, and embracing the rabbinacy during the difficult years of reconstruction at Yavneh.

It is entirely possible that the mystery of manna passed to the rabbinacy by the same route. If Matthew is to be trusted, the Pharisees were ignorant of the mystery. Rabbinic tradition was not ignorant, and 4 Ezra is indicative of a trajectory within Judaism by which the mystery may have been transmitted.

When, following the disastrous defeat of the Bar Kochbah rebellion in 132–135 C.E., the rabbinacy lost patience with active messianism, Jewish mystics who remained within the rabbinacy radically limited the range of their interests.[3] Much that had interested the apocalyptists was no longer made the subject of visions.[4] The stories, however, continued to be told.

Midrash was the genre of rabbinic commentary on the narrative portions of the Bible. During the period from the second through the sixth centuries when the canon laws (halakhot) of the Talmud were compiled, midrash was exclusively an oral tradition; but the following centuries saw the collection and publication of the tales. Most were recorded as anonymous traditional commentaries on particular verses of Scripture. Some were recorded in multiple variants.

Many midrashic references to manna restrict themselves to biblical motifs and so provide no indication whether their authors had independent knowledge of the esoteric meanings of the motifs. In a few cases, however, rabbinic expansions of the legend of manna added to the esoterica.

One tradition, known already in the first century, concerns the flavor of manna. Summarizing over a dozen variants of the tale, Ginzberg wrote:

> Manna also showed its heavenly origin in the miraculous flavor it possessed. There was no need of cooking or baking it, nor did it require any other preparation, and still it contained the flavor of every conceivable dish. One had only to desire a certain dish, and no sooner had he thought of it, than manna had the flavor of the dish desired. The same food had a different taste to every one who partook of it, according to his age; to the little children it tasted like milk, to the strong youths like bread, to the old men like honey, to the sick like barley steeped in oil and honey.[5]

The flavors mentioned in this tale are, except for milk, those of the ingredients of the showbread: bread, honey, barley, and oil. Presumably the recipe could employ milk rather than water as the fluid to bind the flour.

It is also notable that this small and highly specific group of flavors were named as illustrations of the claim that manna possessed "the flavor of every conceivable dish." The motif is not fabulous or impossible. Manna possessed every conceivable flavor in that it was able to produce unitive experiences. An experience of the All necessarily included every conceivable flavor.

Rabbinic tradition related a notable conception of the relation of manna to dew. Drawing primarily on Mekhilta Yoma 75b, the medieval Bible commentator Rashi summarized the midrashic variants as follows:

> "There was a layer of dew" [Exod.16:13]. The dew lay on the manna. At another place [Num. 9:9], it says "And when the dew came down," and so forth ["upon the camp at night, the manna fell upon it"]. The dew fell upon the ground and the manna fell upon it, and then dew returned and fell upon it. Behold, it was as though it were carefully packed in a chest.[6]

Because the ark of the covenant was a gold-plated wooden chest, the Mekhilta implied that the manna in the Ark had dew both above and below it. The image suggests that manna was soluble in water.

It is also notable that apart from Moses and Elijah, who is to restore manna in the end times, Jeremiah was the only prophet whom rabbinic tradition associated with manna.

> To serve future generations as a tangible proof of the infinite power of God, the Lord bade Moses lay an earthen vessel full of manna before the Holy Ark, and this command was carried out by Aaron in the second year of the wanderings through the desert. When, many centuries later, the prophet Jeremiah exhorted his contemporaries to study the Torah, and they answered his exhortations, saying, "How shall we then maintain ourselves?" the prophet brought forth the vessel with manna, and spoke to them, saying: "O generation, see ye the word of the Lord; see what it was that served your fathers as food when they applied themselves to the study of the Torah. You, too, will God support in the same way, if you will but devote yourselves to the study of the Torah."[7]

Whether rabbinic tradition, like 2 Maccabees, depended on a historical memory of Jeremiah's role in transmitting the initiatory tradition or, as is perhaps less likely, drew the appropriate exegetical inferences from Jeremiah's book, midrash rightly associated Jeremiah with manna.

The impression that rabbinic midrash only rarely intended manna as a psychoactive sacrament is corroborated by other approaches to rabbinic mysticism. In midrash from the third century onward, when the Israelites heard Yahveh speak the first two commandments at Mount Sinai, they died, only to be immediately resurrected by the divine dew of the Torah. In a survey of the variants of this midrash, Ira Chernus recognized that rabbinic tradition interpreted the Sinai revelation as an occasion of initiatory death.[8] In the present connection, I would draw attention to the "one and only one tradition in rabbinic literature which states directly that the Israelites at Sinai heard God's word directly and yet were not harmed."[9] Chernus translated it as follows:

> R. Johanan said: The voice would go forth and be split into seven voices and from seven voices into seventy languages so

that all the nations would hear, and each and every nation would hear in the language of that nation and their souls would expire, but Israel would hear and not be harmed. How did the voice go forth? R. Tanhuma said: It was two-faced, and it would go forth and murder the nations who did not accept the Torah, but it would give life to Israel who accepted the Torah. This is what Moses said to them after forty years: "For who is there of all flesh that has heard the voice of the living God as we have speaking out of the midst of the fire and has lived?" (Deut. 5:23). You heard His voice and remained alive, but the nations would hear it and die. Come and see how the voice would go forth in Israel's case—to each and every one according to his power. The old men would hear the voice according to their power and the young men according to their power and the infants according to their power and the women according to their power and even Moses according to his power, as it is said, "Moses spoke and God answered him in thunder [literally, "in a voice"]" (Exod. 19:19). In a voice that Moses would be able to endure. And so it says, "The voice of the Lord in power." It does not say "in His power" but "in power"—so that each and every one would be able to endure it. And even the pregnant women according to their power; so you must say, each and every one according to his power. R. Jose b. Hanina said: If it surprises you, look at the example of the manna which only fell for Israel according to the power of each and every one of them. The young men would eat it as if it were bread . . . and the old men as a wafer with honey. . . and the infants as milk from their mother's breasts . . . and the sick as fine flour mixed with honey . . . but to the nations it would taste as bitter as coriander . . . R. Jose b. Hanina said: If the manna, which was of one species, was transformed for them into many species according to the needs of each and every one, how much more so was it true of the voice which went forth and had power that it was transformed for each and every one according to his power so that it would not harm him?[10]

Chernus's analysis of the different traditions that an ancient editor brought together to create this midrash established that the editor drew on existing traditions that spoke of the danger and undesirability of the Sinai revelation. By stringing the traditions together, the editor deliberately reversed their meaning.[11]

The Sinai revelation was claimed to have been adjusted in power to each recipient, precisely as the manna had been.

Importantly, one of the traditions that was woven into this narrative reads as follows:

> R. Simon said: The word would go forth in a two-faced way. It was a life-giving drug for Israel, but a death-dealing drug for the nations of the world. A life-giving drug for Israel: "As you have heard and lived"—you heard and remained alive. But a death-dealing drug for the nations of the world—they heard and died.[12]

The explicit reference to drugs was deleted in the abbreviated use that was made of the tradition in connection with manna, but the allusion would not have been lost on traditional Jewish students of midrash.

The majority tradition of the rabbis that the Israelites died and resurrected in response to the Sinai revelation utilized a motif, apparently introduced by Philo,[13] that contrasted the senses and the mind as mortal and immortal, respectively. Commenting on the deaths of Nadab and Abihu in Lev. 10:1–3, Philo interpreted their actions as a contemplative avoidance of the senses while pursuing intellectual abstractions. This movement within the soul from the realm of bodily death to the domain of eternal life was termed a death and resurrection, not only in Philo, but also in Paul (1 Cor. 15:35–36, 42–44, 49–53) and the majority rabbinic tradition.[14]

A minority tradition instead held that the Sinai revelation of the Torah was, like the manna, a life-giving drug for Israel, but death-dealing to the Gentiles.

SIX

Pseudo-Hierotheos

$\mathcal{M}$ost of the infrequent references to manna by the Fathers of the Christian Church adhered to one of three literary contexts. All were anti-Semitic. The supercession of Judaism by Christianity was often argued by listing manna, along with quail and water, as miraculous provisions of food and drink that the Israelites received in the wilderness. The list of miracles was then used as evidence of the Israelites' faithlessness in making the golden calf and the validity of God's rejection of the Jews in favor of Christianity. This group of patristic references to manna contains no indication that the authors regarded manna as other than a nourishing foodstuff.

A second group of references contrasted manna with the Christian Eucharist. The passages stated that the Israelites ate the manna and died, but Christians eat the Host and live forever. Because of the contrast between manna with Christ's body in these references, it is again untenable that the authors were cognizant of the biblical mystery.

Manna met approval in a third group of references that treated the manna as a type of Christ. The passages stated that just as manna descended from heaven, so Jesus, the bread of life, descended from heaven. The tendency of these references was again anti-Semitic and triumphalist. Because the manna prefigured Christ, the authors implied, Christianity might appropriate the miracle as its own and disallow Jewish claims to divine favor. Once again, the patristic teaching was inconsistent with an esoteric awareness of the continuity of the biblical mystery from Moses through Jesus and the New Testament authors.

I have located only one patristic writer who seems to have known of the mystery of manna. Saint Irenaeus, bishop of Lyons in France, was active in the last quarter of the second century.[1] Irenaeus wrote:

> And He fed them with manna that they might receive food for their souls, as also Moses says in Deuteronomy, "And fed thee with manna, which thy fathers did not know, that thou mightest know that man doeth not live by bread alone; but by every word of God proceeding out of His mouth doth man live." And it enjoined love to God, and taught just dealing towards our neighbor, that we should neither be unjust nor unworthy of God, who prepares man for His friendship through the medium of the Decalogue.[2]

Irenaeus openly stated that the manna of the Israelites was "food for their souls" and he emphasized its psychoactive effect to produce love for God and moral behavior toward other people, in accordance with the teachings of the Mosaic Decalogue. These emphases should be understood in the context of Irenaeus's discussion of Marcus, a Gnostic who had flourished in the middle of the second century. Irenaeus alleged:

> Over a cup mixed with wine he pretends to pray and, whilst greatly prolonging the invocation, he contrives that it should appear purple and red so that Grace, who belongs to the company of those who are superior to all things, may seem to be dropping her blood into that cup by means of his invocation, and that those present should fervently desire to taste of that cup in order that the Grace called hither by that magician may let (her blood) flow into them. Again, he gives to women cups already mixed and full, and bids them offer thanks in his presence. . . .
> And the woman, deluded and puffed up by what has been said, and excited by the expectation that she is about to prophesy, takes the risk, and with her heart pounding abnormally she utters ridiculous nonsense, anything that happens to come into

her head, idly and audaciously, for she is stimulated by a vain
spirit . . . henceforth considers herself as a prophetess, and
thanks Marcus who has shared with her his Grace. She tries to
repay him, not only with the gift of her possessions . . . but also
by physical intercourse, prepared as she is to be united with him
in everything in order that she, with him, may enter the One.[3]

Although Irenaeus stated that he depended for his information
on the confessions of penitent women, he failed to acknowledge
that Marcus, a disciple of Valentinus, was almost certainly administering the cup of his Gnostic eucharist.

Irenaeus understood clearly the distinction between the sacramental use of psychoactive substances and the doctrines with
which they were mixed. Where manna had been used to encour-
age the Israelites to love God and to deal justly with their fellows,
Marcus used a psychoactive substance in a heretical manner to
promote vainglory and libertinism. Marcus was presumably attempting to imitate Jesus' transformation of water into wine;
whether he employed the same psychoactive substance is unclear.
He may have reverted to the mandrake or henbane of the wine of
the Dionysian mysteries.

The major patristic writers were apparently otherwise ignorant
of the mystery of manna. Knowledge of the psychedelic sacrament survived, however, in the Syriac Church. The pseudony-
mous *Book of Hierotheos,* written possibly in the sixth century,
outlines a Syriac Christian mystical practice that was surrounded
with some secrecy. Seeking to die and be reborn with Christ, the
mystics cultivated visions in which they beheld themselves crucified.[4] As I understand the text, the practice outlined in The *Book
of Hierotheos* involved the use of a psychoactive substance in the
Eucharist, followed by the ritual enactment of Jesus' death, burial,
and resurrection as means by which to guide the drug experience
through ecstatic death to mystical union.

The fifth-century Syriac mystic who wrote in Greek under the
name of Dionysius the Areopagite claimed, as a contemporary
and student of Paul's, to have also had a teacher named Hierotheos.[5]
Presumably subsequent to the successful circulation of Pseudo-

Dionysius's writings, another Syrian author sought to capitalize on Pseudo-Dionysius's fame by issuing a book under the name of Hierotheos.[6] The author was possibly Stephen bar-Sudhaile (fl. 500–520).[7] The translator of the *Book of Hierotheos*, F. S. Marsh, stated that

> it seems to have been in constant, if secret, use as a "Mystic's Guide" for more than thirteen centuries. Its authorship was a subject of discussion at the end of the eighth century; it was accounted worthy of a long commentary by a Jacobite patriarch of Antioch at the end of the ninth century; to find a copy of it was the eager desire of a monk of Mosul in the middle of the thirteenth century . . . and Bar-Hebraeus, who was able after diligent seeking to fulfil the monk's desire, was himself fascinated by the book . . . and re-issued it in a revised and annotated edition; in spite of the greater popularity of the "abridged" edition of Bar-Hebraeus, new copies of the original were made in the seventeenth and eighteenth centuries; . . . it was still being bought and sold and read by Syriac ecclesiastics in the middle of the nineteenth century.[8]

Marsh understood the book as a "Story of the Ascent of the Mind" that was based partly on experience, partly on the testimony of other mystics, but largely "on evidence derived, by patient though misdirected study, from the books which he reckoned as 'divine Scriptures.'"[9] In my view, the book is not a story but a manual, and its account of the mind's ascent pertains to a practice that was both ritual and ecstatic.

In keeping with the Christianized Neoplatonism of Pseudo-Dionysius, Pseudo-Hierotheos assigned theological priority to "the hidden Silence and mystic Quiet which destroys the senses and abolishes forms" in "that perfect and original Unification . . . with the essential Supreme Good."[10] His book, however, was much more concerned with angelic matters.

In *The Celestial Hierarchy*, Pseudo-Dionysius had provided the following account of the procedure of envisioning angels.

> Let us, then, call upon Jesus, the Light of the Father, the "true light enlightening every man coming into the world," "through whom we have obtained access" to the Father, the light which

is the source of all light. To the best of our abilities . . . we
should behold the intelligent hierarchies of heaven. . . . We
must lift up the immaterial and steady eyes of our minds to
that outpouring of Light which is so primal, indeed much
more so, and which comes from that source of divinity, I mean
the Father. This is the Light which, by way of representative
symbols, makes known to us the most blessed hierarchies
among the angels. But we need to rise from this outpouring of
illumination so as to come to the simple ray of Light itself.[11]

Pseudo-Dionysius recommended visualizing celestial angels in
symbolic fashion as beings of light in order to induce visions that
came from Jesus and culminated in the unity of divine light.
These imaginative experiences of anthropomorphic beings of
light were to be regarded as "representative symbols," that is, as
mental images that served metaphorically to convey ideas about
the purely "intelligent" or abstract conceptual realities of the
angels. The experience of Jesus as "the simple ray of Light itself"
was similarly to be understood not literally but metaphorically. In
The Ecclesiastical Hierarchy, Pseudo-Dionysius referred to Jesus as
"transcendent mind, utterly divine mind."[12]

The general tendency of Pseudo-Dionysius's Christian
Neoplatonism was to urge mystics to reject, as products of their
own imaginations, all mental images that they beheld during
visions. Visions were compromises of the duality of body and
spirit. They portrayed intelligible realities in sensible forms by
reworking memories of sense perceptions as metaphors. Only the
abstract intellectual meaning of the metaphors was truly spiritual.
Visionary images were experiences partly of grace, but partly of
bodily imagination. Purely spiritual experiences, such as unitive
mysticism, were much to be preferred.

Pseudo-Hierotheos advocated a related but different approach
to visionary practice. From the composition of 1 Enoch in the
third century B.C.E. through the practices of the medieval *hekhalot*
mystics, Jewish visionaries sought to envision the heavenly palace,
angelic service, and throne room of God.[13] The angelic service, in
whose performance the visionary joined, was regarded as the

prototype of the priestly service of the Jerusalem temple.[14] The New Testament attests amply to the importance of this visionary scenario at the origin of Christianity,[15] and it is possible to see several trends in subsequent Christian spirituality as historical derivatives of the mystical ascensions of ancient Judaism. The doctrine that the heavenly service of the angels is the prototype of the priestly service on earth, which is already to be found in the Old Testament,[16] appears in the Benedictine Rule with reference to the Eucharist.[17] In The *Book of Hierotheos*, the Eucharist was similarly viewed as an occasion for participation in the heavenly service of the angels. I suggest, however, that the Syriac practice was not a question of imagining the angelic service while engaging in an earthly rite, but rather of participating within the angelic service both mystically and sacramentally. A monk was to engage in a mystical ascension to God during the performance of the divine office in church.

In conformance with Pseudo-Dionysius's division of the mystical way into the ways of purgation, illumination, and union, Pseudo-Hierotheos designated the purgative stage of the process of mystical ascension as the Mystery of the Cross. It was not purgative in the more common sense of preparatory moral reform and ascesis; rather, it was itself a mystical experience. Pseudo-Hierotheos wrote: "Those who desire to ascend above our world, must (first) unify the Good Nature that is in them with itself; for unless they remove Opposition from its dwelling place, it may be found to be still persisting . . . in the Region where there (can) be no Opposition."[18] Purgation was necessary because the alternative was an interruption of the process of ascension. "I myself have seen many (ascending) Minds, which ascended as far as the Cross, but fell because their garments were defiled—now I have called 'defiled garments' the body and soul that are not pure."[19]

Pseudo-Hierotheos briefly epitomized the purgative process before explaining its features in closer detail. The epitome serves to provide an overview.

When the Ascent takes place, the Body is quiescent as if dead, and the Soul is merged in the Mind—and (yet) in a real sense (the Mind takes the place of) the body, for it dies, as it is written, "that it may live again unto God." But it leaves upon the earth the body which (came) from the earth, and divinely and holily is made simple; for without movement it is caught up to the firmament, and forgets and is oblivious of everything that is on earth.

Now this, how he was caught up, the Apostle also tells us, saying that he was "caught up even to the third heaven"; and again "even unto Paradise": "that he was caught up" he said, but, on the other hand, of the battle which is made with the Mind over against the firmament, he whom that battle did not befall made no mention. (And this is not surprising) because I have seen many of the Minds (that ascend) against whom this battle was not stirred up, and others suffered very sorely and (only) then passed this firmament.

Now when the Mind is moved to ascend, the three Essences (of demons) are assembled together to overwhelm it; but it is filled with divine strength and wondrous might and "smites its enemies behind it, and delivers them to perpetual shame"; that is to say, it says "then in my distress I will call unto the Lord"; and again "Lord, thou wilt require me of my enemies"; and again "Thou wilt not give to destruction the soul that confesses thee." And (it is) as if now the response were made to it, "I the Lord will answer thee"; and, "When I have strengthened thee, thou shalt praise me"; and the Lord will stretch forth the hand of his loving-kindness and will draw the Mind up to the firmament; and then will be divinely and highly fulfilled unto it those things which were done unto our Lord, and it sees the heavens opened, and the angels of the First Watch in the act of saying to it(?) "Lift up your heads, O ye gates"; and the response is made, "That the King of Honours may come in."[20]

The quiescence of the body should not be taken to refer to an anesthetized condition during a trance. Rather, Pseudo-Hierotheos addressed the sort of oblivion to the sensible world that people may have, for example, when attention is rapt in a book, or music, or ideas during a brainstorm, and so forth. By thinking about the difference between sensible and intelligible realities, it was possible to become self-conscious or mindful of the location of one's sense of self amid the intelligibles. In its role as the location of the sense of self, the mind replaced the body and underwent an ecstatic death. Sensible realities continued to be sense-perceived, but they seemed somewhat unreal or, technically, derealized. There was a forgetfulness of, or inattention to, sensible realities, rather than an anesthetized incapacity to perceive physical sensations.

In this condition, Pseudo-Hierotheos stated, some mystics directly ascended to the One. Others first underwent the intense suffering of the Mystery of the Cross.

In its suffering, the soul had to turn to God for help. Only then did the Lord "draw the Mind up to the firmament," that is, enable it to move beyond the sensible to the intelligible. "The firmament appears to the Mind as a kind of dim light."[21] The soul's suffering, which led to its transition from the sensible to the intelligible, had a biblical precedent. The suffering consisted of "those things that were done unto our Lord." The transition was the resurrection that followed the mind's crucifixion.

The intense suffering is, I suggest, conclusive proof that Pseudo-Hierotheos was not discussing an otherworldly scenario that was to be envisioned during an out-of-body experience. Writing around 690, Isaac of Nineveh claimed that suffering was a consequence of God's anger at the impiety of attempting to behold God before having completed the silencing of the senses.

> Every one . . . causes [God's] anger to blow against him because, before having mortified his members on the earth, i.e. before healing the illness of his deliberations by endurance under the labours and the shame of the cross, he has dared to occupy his mind with the glory of the cross. This is what has been said by the ancient saints: If the mind desires to ascend the cross before the senses have become silent on account of weakness, the anger of God will strike it. . . .
>
> For he who hastens to meditate with his heart vain imaginations concerning future things, while his mind is still stained by reprehensible passions, will be reduced to silence on his way by punishment.[22]

Isaac of Nineveh rejected experiences of ecstatic death as "vain imaginations," whose unpleasantness was a divine response to the mystic's sin of having remained in the body. This testimony, stemming from the Syriac monastic tradition subsequent to Pseudo-Hierotheos, indicates that Pseudo-Hierotheos's Mind was not envisioning its disembodiment amid proceedings in heaven. The Mind knew terror and fear because it was still embodied.

The continued embodiment of the Mind implies that the angels of the First Watch, who spoke at this juncture, are to be understood as other churchmen who were present during the ritual in order to guide and otherwise assist the visionary who was undergoing an ecstatic death. Because Pseudo-Hierotheos wrote in the Pseudo-Dionysian tradition, we may not assume that he regarded angels as anthropomorphic, metaphysical beings who may be seen in visions. We must expect him to have been conversant with the Neoplatonic practice of allegorism. On the other hand, Pseudo-Hierotheos plainly did not intend angels in Pseudo-Dionysius's manner as purely intelligible, spiritual beings. He stated that "the divine Mind," that is, the resurrected and divinized or Christlike mind of the mystical initiate, "is greatly moved and bewildered . . . and it supposes concerning those angels that they are those who have reached the fulfilment of perfect contemplation, and that in them, divinely and highly, the perfect all-fulfilling Fulness is (completely) contained."[23] These words do not describe angels as beings who are endowed with inalienable powers of perfect contemplation in the divine presence. Rather, Pseudo-Hierotheos's angels were imperfect beings who had successfully completed their own ascensions and so had "reached the fulfilment of perfect contemplation." This conception of angels is coherent not only in biblical Hebrew, but also in the cognate Syriac language, where the term *malak*, "messenger," may mean either a human agent, such as a prophet, or a metaphysical being. Inapplicable to metaphysical beings, Pseudo-Hierotheos's references to angels were to be interpreted, I suggest, in terms of mortal human messengers of God.

Pseudo-Hierotheos stated that the angels now taught a secret to the initiate, but he did not tell his reader what that secret was.

"Then those angels are moved to impart to the Mind a mystery of spiritual contemplation, and (so) they explain to it, mystically and divinely, the secret of their charge and the function of their hierarchy."[24] By drawing the reader's attention to the fact that his text concerned a secret, Pseudo-Hierotheos encouraged uninitiated readers to read his text carefully at this juncture.

Having raised the topic of a secret, Pseudo-Hierotheos went on to explain that the angels administered the Eucharist to the initiate.

> Great weariness and toil (are in store) for Minds in the way of the Ascent, and (so) that natural yearning which desires to obtain fulfilment is strengthened in them, and they are aided and helped by the Essence which meets them, by means of the spiritual Bread that is given to them. All (the angels of that Essence) therefore are gloriously and holily gathered together to the Mind in a wonderful mystery.[25]

The following passage explicitly states that the administration of the Eucharist is the angelic labor that brings about the initiate's ascension. Having ascended, the initiate is himself able to serve as an initiator. This attainment was the occasion of an ordination through a laying on of hands by the divine hierarch.

> The work of [the] hierarchy is the advancement of those who are brought near, and the purification of those that are purified; for there can be no unification without one who sanctifies and purifies and cleanses and unites. So the Mind, after it is purified and ascends, acquires also (the power?) to receive and to purify. The divine Hierarch of the first Hierarchy is moved, therefore, to make the Mind partaker in his perfect fulness, so that now it may be sanctifying and purifying those Essences that are united with it; and the divine Mind also approaches and bows its head, mystically and divinely, for that holy and glorious Laying-on-of-hands. . . . Then it is wonderfully and divinely strengthened, and summons those angels, in glorious and divine mystery, to perform with them another mystery . . . of Communion, and distributes to them the living and holy Eucharist; and from the time when it receives the divine Laying-on-of-hands, it becomes no longer one who receives from them, but one who gives to them.[26]

The divine Mind next ascended to a second heavenly mansion,

where it was received by further angels. "It yields itself willingly (to them) and receives from them the 'contemplation' of mysteries through that spiritual Bread whose rank is exalted and whose fame is glorious—but they who receive it must have felt its virtue."[27] With these words Pseudo-Hierotheos let drop the secret of the angelic initiation. The virtue of the angelic bread was not limited to the sacramental significance of the Eucharist rite. The "spiritual Bread" caused the Mind to attain a contemplative state of consciousness. The angelic Eucharist wafer was explicitly psychoactive.

Having partaken of the Eucharist, the initiate proceeded to the Mystery of the Cross.

> Now the divine Mind enters the place, of the sufferings. . . .
> And then it sees divinely the three wonderful and divine and mystic Crosses of marvel; and then it asks "For what purpose are these?" and the response is made to it "These are on account of thee." And when it sees these things, it is disturbed and grieved, and draws near to the Hierarch who is in that place, and learns from him, mystically and holily, the mysteries that are (now to be) accomplished.[28]

The historical Jesus was again claimed as a precedent for the esoteric practice. A mystical initiate did no more than imitate Christ.

> Those who are being divinely made perfect and sublimely sanctified, must in everything acquire the likeness of Christ, and become as he was. . . . Christ himself left the condition of human life by way of the Cross of passions. . . . It is right, therefore, for those divine Minds that wish to become as Christ, that in everything they should be made like him, and in everything become as he was. Else how shall they come to fulfilment?[29]

As proof that the historical Jesus was concerned with experiences of ecstatic death, and not only with a bodily crucifixion on a wooden cross, Pseudo-Hierotheos cited the gospel account of the sons of Zebedee.

> And do not let the significance of (the story of?) the sons of Zebedee escape thee, O my son: when their mother asked of

him "that these my two sons may sit one on they right hand and one of thy left", and he gave to her and to them the complete answer, "Are ye able to drink the cup that I am about to drink?" can he have spoken (merely) of the human Cross?— when this the sons of Zebedee did not bear, neither, indeed, did this passion come to many of those who loved him. (But if he was not speaking of the human Cross), then it is evident to us that he spoke of that Intelligible Cross which divine Minds receive; for they cannot be divinely perfected and mystically sanctified, unless they reach and endure that Cross of passions.[30]

Because the sons of Zebedee were not crucified bodily on crosses of wood, their crucifixion, which was produced by drinking of a cup, had necessarily to consist of an ecstatic death on "that Intelligible Cross which divine Minds receive."

The precedents of Jesus and the sons of Zebedee were Pseudo-Hierotheos's authorities for the ongoing Syriac practice of the Mystery of the Cross. "So it is meet for divine Minds, that they also should slay the body of sin by the holy and mystic Cross."[31]

Pseudo-Hierotheos understood the experience of crucifixion on the "Intelligible Cross" from a perspective that blended the Christian myth of the fall with Neoplatonic ideas of the declension of the intelligible One into the sensible Many.

Do not thou then, my son, when thou reachest the Cross, suppose and believe that this is already the limit of the House of God, for lo, the divine Bartholomew called it (only) the gate; but who shall enter the city if he reach not the gate, or who shall reach the limit of Goodness (if he take not the first step thereto), or attain to Unification without the Cross? The Cross then, I say, is a kind of purifying and cleansing power, which through passion that causes passion brings passions to an end. Yet know, that if (there had been) no Fall, neither (would there be) passion; and if (there were) no passion, neither (would there be) the Cross. For if the Mind had preserved its Essence, it would not have incurred the Coming (into this life?); and where there is no Coming, neither is there Going. And so it has been made known to us, that the Cross is something necessary not to the Essence of the Mind, but to its purification.[32]

Having fallen into physicality and multiplicity, the human

mind was obliged to undergo purgation of all that it had acquired in the process of its decline, before it could reunite with the One. The Mystery of the Cross was not the ultimate goal of the mystical life, but only its beginning.

Pseudo-Hierotheos described the mind's crucifixion as an experience of terror and fear. "When therefore the Mind sees those Crosses, it is terrified and afraid; and perhaps also its sweat may congeal like drops of blood that in everything it may be made like Him who was made like us."[33] When the initiate began to panic, the chief initiator was to comfort him by encouraging him to trust in his survival. "The Chief of the Angels of that place draws near and presents to it that comforting assurance which was also presented to Christ, and these are the (words) he says to it, 'The time is swift and very short, and then thou shalt be glorified: despise death that thou mayest live.'"[34]

Departing significantly from the tradition descended from Saint Anthony that attributed experiences of ecstatic death to the enmity of demons, Pseudo-Hierotheos insisted that the visions may portray demons but are nevertheless virtuous in their origin. The sufferings were necessary if mind was to abandon both soul and body.

> But know, O my son, that it is the angels who rise up in that place against the divine Mind and crucify it; and do not suppose or believe that perhaps this glorious service may be accomplished by the Essence of demons: (it is not) demons but (angels who), changing their likeness, play to it the part of Crucifiers.
>
> Now, therefore, that divine Mind draws near to effect the dissolution of its unity, and relinquishes its Soul, and lets go its Body, with sufferings and groanings unutterable.[35]

The abandonment of body and soul permitted the mind to advance toward the One. It "draws near, nakedly, without soul and without body, while Soul and Body remain alone, and surrenders itself in holiness and humility to the Cross of passions."[36] Once again, what was under discussion was a self-consciousness or mindfulness that relocated the sense of self in the mind, as distinct from in the soul or the body. This relocation was accomplished by visualizing vivid, pictorial, mental images of being crucified on a cross. "It is crucified on the middle Cross, and it sees the Soul, too, on its right hand, crucified like Titus, and the Body, like Zumachus, on its left hand—and because it is Christ it is meet that it should be crucified (?) in the middle."[37] The visualized images were to be interpreted in a fashion consistent with the teachings of Pseudo-Dionysius. Although an initiate visualized himself as Christ, crucified between Titus and Zumachus, he was to understand these mental images as allegories that symbolized the crucifixion of his mind, soul, and body.

Having performed the requisite visualizations, the initiate was to await the transformation of the mental images into an experience of ecstatic death.

> Then will come the hour of death which is inseparable from the Cross . . . and the divine Mind will cry out and say, "O God, O God, why has thou forsaken me?" and will bow its head in great humiliation, and will endure the mystical Death, by which, in Christ, it is appointed that we should die—for no one can become Christ whosoever dies not by this death—and the Body also and the Soul die with it.[38]

At this point in the proceedings, features of the crucifixion of Jesus were to be enacted by the company of initiators.

> Now some of the angels possess the sign, as it were, of Attendants, and some perform the work of the Soldiers; and one of them draws near, mystically and divinely, and seems to pierce the Mind, in its side, with the sign, as it were, of a spear which is in his hand, and, mystically and holily, causes to flow the sign (as it were) of blood and of water; and (one) like Joseph the Councillor seems to take down the divine Mind from the all-holy and mystical Cross. . . . and then they bring it, mystically and divinely, to the Tomb of divine mystery.[39]
>
> Pseudo-Hierotheos intended an experience during which sense perception and bodily actions were possible. After remarking that Paul referred to "the mystical Death of Minds"[40] when he said "He who is dead has been set free from sin" (Romans 6:7), Pseudo-Hierotheos explained the Pauline concept of burial as continence.

> And do thou, when thou hearest the Apostle, our Teacher,
> (say) death, think of that divine Death which divine Minds
> undergo at the time of the Cross; and if thou hearest (him say)
> burial, (think) of that wondrous and divine and intelligible
> Burial, which the Apostle, our Teacher, named "the Tomb of
> Continence", when he commands us, highly and divinely, to be
> in the Tomb of Continence.[41]

Because it is not meaningful to be continent unless the possibility
of incontinence exists, it is necessary to conclude that the burial
proceeded during a potentially active, waking state when both
moral and immoral actions were possible.

Burial was simultaneously the content of a dramatic rite in
which the initiate enacted the part of the historical Jesus. Burial
involved a change of location within the church, but it was
performed by the same initiators, who now took the role of the
Disciples.

> Concerning the Essence of that Tomb and whence it is, per-
> haps it is right to say (a word); and, for my own part, I say that
> it is a definite and distinct position prepared in the place of the
> Cross, which undergoes as it were a certain change at the time
> when the Mind has been laid in it. And concerning those who
> bury (the Mind), I say that they are of the same glorious Rank
> of angels who minister in the place of the Cross; perhaps, also,
> they display some token of mourning at the time when the
> Mind is buried; that is to say, they fulfil for it as it were the part
> of the Disciples.[42]

When the mind emerged from the tomb, its initiators were to
be dressed in white garments as angels.

> When the mind, therefore, has spent three days in the Tomb,
> it must next fulfil the mystery of the Resurrection. Now there-
> fore it awakes in power and in might, and perhaps also it will
> see angels, in white garments, proclaiming its glorious resur-
> rection; and others, again, holily and divinely rolling the stone
> from the door (of the tomb).[43]

Having fully grasped, by means of his visionary ordeal, the
mind's integrity apart from soul and body, the communicant was
to effect his mind's resurrection by returning his sense of self to

his soul and body. An increased capacity for self-consciousness or mindfulness would remain, however, as a permanent consequence of the experience.

> When it has awakened, it sees divinely, and understands highly, that it is no longer living the life of the body, but that wonderful and marvellous life that is not liable to variation; and it sees itself without body and without soul, and this is what it says, "It is right for me now to bring a resurrection to pass for the Essences that were with me and in me." And so it stretches out the bountiful hand of its goodness, to bring to life the Body and the Soul. And when it does this, it still remains separate from them, and therefore it begins to make that unification with them, which, before the Cross, it dissolved. . . . and so the Mind puts on its Soul and its Body, since it sees that they have become bright and even beautiful in comparison with what they were before the Cross. And then it begins to purify and to cleanse the Soul and the Body that have been made one with it.[44]

The glorification of the resurrected mind entailed, among other things, a ritual investiture with a white garment consistent with the transfiguration of Jesus in the Gospels. The communicant now began to recognize the access that he had gained to divine illumination.

> Then that Good Nature begins to burst forth, and highly and divinely appears as a glorious and flashing fiery fierceness, which flames divinely and is holily enkindled; and therein is fulfilled the Word which says, "We shall become in the likeness of the glorious body of Christ"; and it is transfigured in the sight of the angels that are in that place, as also Christ (was transfigured) in the sight of the Disciples on the mountain. For, highly and divinely, they see that its face is ten thousand times more radiant than the sun, and its garment whiter than snow; and perhaps thereby is fulfilled the Word which says, "In thy light do we see light, and are enabled to be enlightened.". . . And now (the Mind) is transformed, when its mortality is swallowed up in life, and its darkness in light; and perhaps it wonders at its own self.[45]

Following the mind's glorification, the communicant "begins sublimely to experience divine Unification. . . . and it rejoices also, highly and divinely, at the wonderful unity of its glorious light."[46]

The transition of the ecstasy into a euphoric experience of mystical union was termed a baptism. Having achieved union with Christ, the initiate was no longer called "Mind," but "Christ."

> The Baptism with water is the Baptism of the body, and (that) it is only a symbol and type of the glorious and real Baptism, of which all divine Minds are accounted worthy in the place that is above the heavens. . . . the Mind also consents to draw near to that holy Baptism, and is divinely and holily baptized with that holy and glorious Baptism; and then is revealed to it, divinely and holily, that mystery which was revealed to the Baptist in Him-who-was-baptized; and it sees again the Holy Spirit coming upon it in the bodily likeness of a dove; and now it has nothing at all to prevent it from becoming in everything like Christ, and so it puts away the designation of "Mind," and is called "Christ."[47]

Following his baptism, the initiate dispensed the spiritual Eucharist to the angels. Presumably because there was no further risk of the initiate having a psychological crisis, the initiators could afford to relax their vigilant sobriety and join the novice in an ecstatic state.

> And then, the divine Mind which has become Christ is brought near to perform the mystery that is appropriate, and to give the glorious Fragment of the spiritual Eucharist to the Host that is above the heavens; in order that . . . it may divinely help the Essences by which it was helped and strengthened and supported at the time of its Ascent; and the Powers that help (Minds) to ascend are gathered together and look towards it.[48]

Pseudo-Hierotheos regarded the wafer and water of the public Christian Eucharist as symbols of the psychedelic substances of the secret Eucharist.

> Know, O my son, that this material and bodily bread which is set upon the material altar is a kind of perceptible sign—and, to tell the truth, a small and unworthy shadow—of that glorious Bread which is above the heavens; and the cup of mixture also that is in our world—it too, is (only) a material sign of that glorious and holy Drink of which the Mind is accounted worthy in the place that is above.[49]

Pseudo-Hierotheos continued with Neoplatonic interpretations of a variety of mystical experiences. Mystical contemplation
proceeded ultimately to a complete transcendence of all images.
"The divine Mind is exalted as far as (the place) where it finds
'appearance' no more; and it also says, 'There is no appearance
before my eyes.'"[50] This mysticism of the One was consistent with
the negative theology of Pseudo-Dionysius. Pseudo-Hierotheos
wrote:

> Everything becomes One Thing: for even God shall pass, and
> Christ shall be done away, and the Spirit shall no more be
> called the Spirit,—for names pass away and not Essence; for if
> distinction pass, who will call whom? and who, on the other
> hand, will answer whom? for One neither names nor is named.
> This is the limit of All and the end of Everything.[51]

Although the transcendent One was ultimate, unitive experiences dealt with the universal and were consequently penultimate.
"It burns, holily and divinely, in spiritual contemplation, to come
to the Tree of Life, and to be united with it. These things it does
with divine comprehension and mystical understanding of the
significance of its journey; and so, in glory (most) glorified, it
arrives at the Essence which is called 'Universal.'"[52]

Union with the universal essence was also the ideology that
Pseudo-Hierotheos attached to experiences of inspiration. "The
members of the Universal Essence begin wonderfully to declare
to that divine Mind the glorious mystery of their divine ministry;
nor, indeed, thenceforward, O my son, would they be able to
withhold from the Mind their high and divine knowledge, seeing
that now it has been divinely united with them (so that it and
they are) one."[53]

SEVEN

Medieval Rabbinic Authorities

*B*etween the ninth and thirteenth centuries, when Hellenic learning was revived in the Islamicate, a series of rabbis and scholars transformed Judaism by placing its teachings on a rational basis. The most important figures of the period were community leaders who were widely acknowledged as authoritative experts in the traditional topics of Bible, Talmud, and midrash. These men additionally wrote the first Jewish philosophies since the time of Philo of Alexandria, articulated Hebrew philology and grammar, penned commentaries on the Bible and Talmud, codified Jewish law, and presented Jewish mysticism in a systematic fashion.

A subset of the medieval rationalizers of Judaism wrote esoterically of the mystery of manna. They included Saadia Gaon, Rashi, and Rambam (Maimonides), three of the half dozen most illustrious rabbis in the history of Judaism.

Considered from a literary perspective, the medieval contributions added a new complexity to the literature. In addition to the traditional creation of esoteric subtexts through metaphor, allegory, and incomplete statements, these authors concealed secrets in more complex manners that were influenced by the literary techniques of the alchemists.[1] They borrowed Jabir's technique of dispersion, by which esoteric discussions were divided into incomplete pieces that were located at irregular intervals within a book. Readers were obliged to treat the books as though their passages were pieces of a jigsaw puzzle, to be fitted together in different orders than their literary presentation. The medieval style of Jewish esotericism also relied heavily on misdirection. The texts referred obliquely to secrets while seeming to discuss innocuous exoteric topics.

Saadia Gaon

Rabbi Saadia ben Joseph (882–942), Gaon of the rabbinic academy in Sura, Babylonia, was the most important figure of tenth-century Judaism. In addition to his work as head of the academy and de facto chief rabbi of international Jewry, Saadia pioneered Hebrew grammatical studies, translated the Hebrew Bible into Arabic, composed a partial commentary on the Bible, introduced the writing of monographs on halakhic (legal) decisions, composed liturgical poems, and organized the Jewish prayer book (in Arabic). He encouraged Jewish contributions to mathematics, astronomy, and other physical sciences, and he wrote the oldest work of medieval Jewish philosophy that survives intact. His philosophy belonged to the eclectic tradition of the Mutazilite school of the Muslim Kalamists. It was intended not as a complete system, but specifically to rationalize biblical and talmudic law.[2]

In Saadia's major philosophic work, *The Book of Beliefs and Opinions*, he referred to manna in a distinctive manner that indicates the presence of a subtext.

> When, furthermore, He says: *And ye are My witnesses* (Isa. 44:8), He alludes to the marvelous signs and the manifest proofs witnessed by the [Jewish] people. . . . Personally . . . I consider the case of the miracle of the manna as the most amazing of all miracles, because a phenomenon of an enduring nature excites greater wonderment than one of a passing character. Aye it is hard for the mind to conceive of a scheme whereby a people numbering something like two million souls could be nourished for forty years with nothing else than food produced for them in the air by the Creator. For had there

> been any possibility of thinking up a scheme for achieving
> something of this nature, the philosophers of old would have
> been the first to resort to it. They would have maintained their
> disciples therewith, taught them wisdom, and enabled them to
> dispense with working for a livelihood or asking for help.[3]

In calling manna "a phenomenon of an enduring nature," did Saadia refer only to the forty years that the Israelites ate manna in the wilderness? Or did he also intend to allude to its endurance down to his own time? The answer is given in the sequel. After remarking that two million souls availed themselves of manna as a food supply, Saadia did not go on to suggest that people in general would have availed themselves of manna as a food supply. He changed the topic, for no apparent reason, and referred suddenly to "the philosophers of old" and "their disciples." The abrupt transition brought the miracle of manna into association with the chain of transmission within the philosophic tradition. Although Saadia's tone implied that the philosophers made no use of manna, his literal wording conveys an opposite implication; and his tone may be ignored as a misdirection. The clause "taught them wisdom" in the final sentence is gratuitous and intrusive, unless Saadia meant that the disciples' maintenance by means of manna was the means by which they were taught wisdom.

A second and, in my view, conclusive reference to manna occurs in passing much later in the book, in the course of a discussion of the resurrection of the dead. Saadia began by remarking that a majority of the Jews maintained that the resurrection would occur in this world at the time of the redemption, while a minority opinion, which he rejected, held that it would occur in the world to come. Saadia then turned to discuss the circumstances under which it was permissible to interpret the Bible allegorically. These circumstances were four in number. In the first, a statement might be inconsistent with the evidence of the senses; for example, *"And the man called his wife's name Eve; because she was the mother of all living* (Gen. 3:20), whereas we see that the ox and the lion are not the offspring of womankind."[4]

An allegorical reading was also permissible whenever a biblical statement was inconsistent with reason. For example, "*For the Lord thy God is a devouring fire, a jealous God* (Deut. 4:24). Now fire is something created and defective, for it is subject to extinction."[5]

Internal contradictions in Scripture constituted a third circumstance that made allegorical readings permissible. It was in this connection that Saadia referred to manna.

> Thus, for example, it is said in Scripture: *Ye shall not try the Lord your God, as ye tried Him in Massah* (Deut. 6:16). And it is also said, on the other hand: *And try Me now herewith . . . if I will not open you the windows of heaven* (Mal. 3:10). Now the point wherein these two statements agree is that we must not test our Lord as to whether He is able to do a certain thing, as they did of whom it is reported: *And they tried God in their heart by asking food for their craving. Yea, they spoke against God; they said: "Can God prepare a table in the wilderness?"* (Ps. 78:18, 19). It is to these that the remark *as ye tried Him in Massah* refers. It is, however, permissible for a servant to God to test his Master's power by asking whether it be possible for Him to create a miracle in his behalf. Such a request was indeed made by Gideon, who said: *Let me make trial, I pray Thee, but this once with the fleece* (Judg. 6:39). It was also done by Hezekiah (II Kings 20:8) and others.[6]

The final circumstance authorizing allegorical readings was "authentic tradition." Saadia gave the example that the biblical commandment to administer a punishment of forty stripes (Deut. 25:3) was traditionally understood to refer to thirty-nine blows.

> The text of Scripture has merely expressed this thought in round numbers, as it has done in the statement: *After the number of the days in which ye spied out the land, even forty days, for every day a year shall ye bear your iniquities, even forty years* (Num. 14:34). For in reality there were only thirty-nine years, since the first year of Israel's sojourn in the wilderness did not enter into this punishment.[7]

Saadia conveyed an esoteric subtext through his selection of biblical verses to illustrate his argument on methodology. His assimilation of the trial at Massah to the trial of manna exemplifies the mode of esoteric interpretation to be employed throughout the passage; the biblical verses are all to be interpreted in terms of a single esoteric topic. Manna's association with Massah, where Moses produced water by striking a rock, identifies the esoteric topic in question.

The keys to the subtext in this passage occur, however, in yet other locations within Saadia's book. In keeping with the tradition of Hebrew biblical theology that reached Philo and the Johannine Gospel, Saadia maintained that the image of God that the prophets beheld in visions was a phenomenon created by God for the purpose of conveying revelations.

> The [sense of] sight has no power to perceive Him . . . even imagination has no means of picture or forming an image of God. . . .
>
> Now some people are confused by the story related in Scripture that our teacher Moses requested of His Master: *Show me, I pray Thee, Thy glory* (Exod. 33:18). . . .
>
> I say, then, invoking the aid of God in the effort to reveal and clarify all this, that God has a special light which He creates and makes manifest to His prophets in order that they may infer therefrom that it is a prophetic communication emanating from God that they hear. When one of them sees this light, he says, "I have seen *the glory of the Lord*." Often, however, he would say simply: "I have seen God," by way of ellipsis.[8]

In yet another passage, Saadia identified the living creatures of the divine chariot that Ezekiel beheld with popular notions concerning the angel of death.

> Our forebears have informed us that the angel who is dispatched by the Creator for the purpose of separating the soul and the body appears to man in the form of a figure of yellowish fire filled with eyes composed of bluish fire and holding in his hand a drawn sword aimed at him. Upon seeing him thus, the person shudders and his spirit separates from his body. . . .
>
> I furthermore found support for the view that the body of the angel is composed of a yellowish fire in the statement of Scripture: *As for the likeness of the living creatures, their appearance was like coals of fire, burning like the appearance of torches* (Ezek 1:13).[9]

There was no rabbinic precedent for Saadia's association of the angel of death with the chariot of the glory. The association is consistent, however, with the knowledge that visionary experiences of the glory included the occurrence of ecstatic deaths. Much as Saadia publicly affirmed belief in a resurrection of the dead at the time of the redemption, his subtext concerned experiences of ecstatic death. Saadia adduced that Eve was the mother of all living in order to intimate that resurrection occurs to the living (cf. Matt. 22:31–32). The reconstitution of corpses was not under discussion. Saadia next cited a text stating that God is a devouring fire, only to deny its validity in order to allude to the fiery and frightening appearance of the angel of death. Third, the notion of a trial, in whose connection Saadia mentioned manna, was implicitly offered in explanation of ecstatic death experiences. Indeed it was permissible, Saadia intimated, to ask God for a miracle. One did so by eating manna in implicit request of revelations. Saadia's remark that Hezekiah had tried God alluded to a famous talmudic story in which Rabbi Yochanan ben Zakkai referred to the messiah as "Hezekiah, king of Judah, who comes."[10] Saadia meant that a public trial of manna, consistent with the effort in the era of Hezekiah, Isaiah, and the Priestly author, was to be expected of the future Son of David. Lastly, Saadia's assertion that forty approximated the number of stripes that were to be inflicted in punishment introduced the notions of approximation and punishment. Ecstatic death was to be understood as a punitive experience; but its manifestation precisely as a vision of the angel of death was only an approximation of the many forms taken by real experiences.

Future research will be needed to decide whether it is significant that Saadia referred to "the philosophers of old" rather than to a chain of rabbinic transmission. From the ninth through the twelfth century, the philosophers of the Arabic-speaking world were often in conversation with each other, regardless of whether they were Muslim, Jewish, Christian, Hermetic, or Zoroastrian. In such a context, it is not impossible that the biblical mystery of manna provided a basis for ecumenical contacts.

Rashi

Rabbi Solomon ben Isaac (1040–1105), traditionally known by his acronym RaShI, was born in Troyes, the capital of the province of Champagne in northeastern France. Following his marriage, he was educated at the great rabbinic academies in Mainz and Worms. He returned to Troyes around 1065 and there founded a rabbinic academy in 1070, which he headed until his death. Like Saadia, Rashi was one of the giants of medieval Judaism, and his intellectual contribution has remained current. Rashi's running commentaries on the Bible and large portions of the Talmud have for centuries been the standard commentaries in which Jewish children are educated, and from which all more advanced discussion begins. Rashi's commentaries are distinguished by their philological and grammatical expertise and their devotion to the literal meaning of the texts. Some two hundred commentaries have been written on Rashi's Pentateuch commentary, including one by the distinguished halakhist Joseph Karo, author of the *Shulkhan Arukh*. Rashi's preeminence came to be expressed through his title "Parshandata," "expounder of the law" or "commentator," as though no second merited consideration. Rashi's scattered comments and rabbinic responsa on halakhic questions were also influential among French, German, and Italian Jews.[11]

Some of Rashi's remarks on manna bear close attention. At Exod. 16:3, Rashi commented: "*mutenu*: that we may die; and it is not a noun like *mitatenu*, 'our death,' but like *asotenu, khanotenu, shovenu*, to make us, to encamp us, to make us die."[12]

Rashi composed this passage as though a grammatical discussion were his concern; but the ostensible interest in verb conjugations was a misdirection. Rashi conveyed an esoteric message through his choice of verbs. In Exod. 16:3, the biblical text uses the noun *motenu*, "our death," in a sentence that literally reads, "Would that he gave our deaths at the hand of Yahveh in the land of Egypt." Rashi nevertheless contrived to read the word as *mutenu*, a gerund meaning "our dying," which he explicated in a transitive sense as "the making of us to die." By way of preface to this incorrect and unnecessary bit of grammar, Rashi introduced the notion "that we may die." The verb tense implied a future event. Rashi also mentioned the word *shovenu* as a grammatical parallel without adding its explication, "to make us repent." In place of "to make us repent," he wrote "to make us die." In this manner, he associated manna with both impending death and repentance. The associations appear accidental and insignificant to uninitiated readers. The contrary assumption that they were deliberate permits them to convey an esoteric subject to the understanding of initiated readers.

How may we be certain that Rashi's juxtapositions were not accidental but deliberate? Because his seemingly random juxtapositions convey a coherent message in passage after passage. It is not the coherence of any one passage, but the consistent coherence of passage after passage that establishes Rashi's intentions.

At Exod. 16:7, Rashi commented:

> *u-boqer u-ra'item*, "and morning and you shall see"—Not with regard the Glory of which it is said "And behold, the Glory of [YHV]H is seen in the cloud [Exod. 16:10]", it is said. Rather, he spoke with them this way: [In the] evening, and you shall know that the power is in his hand to give your desire, and he will give meat, but he will not give it to you with a luminous face, because you have asked him inappropriately, and out of a full belly; but [concerning] the bread that you ask for your necessity, in its descent at morning you shall see the glory of the light of his face, in order that it descend to you in the way of love.

Working with the received text of Exodus rather than a modern scholarly analysis of its sources, Rashi distinguished the glory that attended the manna from the glory that was visible immediately following Moses' prophecy of both the quail and the manna. The latter was the glory that manifested as a cloud by day and a pillar of fire by night. The glory that was visible in the morning in conjunction with the manna was the glory of the light of Yahveh's face. In this manner, Rashi emphasized manna's relation to visionary experience and also stressed that the luminous glory was not provided in connection with the quail. The luminous glory was associated with manna exclusively, as proof of God's love.

Similarly, at Exod. 16:33, in recounting the midrashic tale of Jeremiah's exhibition of the manna to the public, Rashi added: "he said to them, 'See the word of the Lord!' He did not say 'Hear!, but 'See! By this your fathers were given their livelihoods. Many messengers the Omnipresent has for him to prepare food for those who fear Him.'"

Rashi drew on Deut. 4:12, where the Israelites are said to have heard God's voice at Sinai. Drawing on a rabbinic source termed the Mekhilta, Rashi adduced the term *shaliah,* "messenger," that was used in the Hebrew Bible with regard to the commissioning of prophets. For Rashi, the midrashic tale of Jeremiah's involvement with manna became the basis for asserting that manna, the visible word of God, was a foodstuff that many prophets had dispensed to the devout. His choice of the term *shaliakh* had an ecumenical significance. He was not thinking exclusively of Hebrew prophets. The Aramaic and Syriac cognates *shalikha* were used technically in Christianity to denote Jesus' apostles, and the Arabic translation *rasul* referred above all to Muhammad.[13]

Rashi's association of manna with both death and repentance, his care in distinguishing the luminous glory from the daily glory in the cloud, and his description of manna as the visible word that prophets feed the devout, attest to a coherent conception of the psychedelic sacrament and the type of religious experience associated with it. His allusions preserved the secrecy of the biblical mystery, but referred to it in a knowing manner that a fellow initiate would find unmistakable.

Rabbi Moses Maimonides

Rabbi Moshe ben Maimon (1135–1204), known in Hebrew by his acronym RaMBaM and to Western Christianity as Moses

Maimonides, was born in Cordoba, Spain. The Almohad conquest of Cordoba in 1148 led to religious persecutions, however, causing Maimon and his sons to relocate. In 1160, they settled in Fez, Morocco, where Moses was exposed to Islamic philosophy and medicine. In 1165, the family landed at Acre and made a tour of the Holy Land before proceeding to Cairo, where Maimonides lived until his death. In Cairo, Maimonides promoted the Rabbanite cause and was pivotal in destroying the domination among the Jews of Cairo by the Karaite sect, which rejected the authority of the rabbinacy. Following the death of his brother David in 1173, Maimonides became a physician. About 1177, Maimonides became the recognized leader of the Jews of Cairo. From 1185 onward, he was a royal physician to the Muslim vizier al-Fadil.

Maimonides was the greatest rabbinic authority of his age and the only man in the history of the medieval rabbinacy to eclipse Saadia Gaon in overall stature. Maimonides' *Mishneh Torah* was the first systematic codification of Jewish law and his *Moreh Nevukhim*, "Guide of the Perplexed," placed Jewish philosophy on firmly Aristotelian principles. It is the single most important philosophic work written by a Jew. It shaped the subsequent course of medieval Jewish philosophy and, centuries later, proved seminal for modern Jewish thought. The *Guide* was also fundamental to medieval Catholicism's turn to Aristotle in the works of Albertus Magnus, Thomas Aquinas, and Meister Eckhart.[14] Maimonides's authority is summarized by the popular Hebrew saying, "From Moses to Moses there is none like Moses."

In his *Guide of the Perplexed*, Maimonides openly announced that he was using esoteric literary techniques in order to conform with the practices of Jewish mystics.[15] Contemporary with the first generation of Kabbalists, Maimonides wrote in an esoteric fashion, I suggest, in order to prove to Jewish esotericians that they had no secrets that he did not know and had not taken into account in developing his philosophy. Elliot R. Wolfson has remarked: "Maimonides is aware of the earlier esoteric traditions and exerted much effort to subvert them by utilizing the key terms ... but investing them with radical new meaning. ... There is very little that is esoteric in the true sense of that term for him; what is esoteric is the style of presentation and the claim that certain matters have been concealed from the public."[16]

Maimonides twice referred to manna in the *Guide*. The first instance occurred in a discussion of the verb *malle'*. The passage is a masterful instance of misdirection. Uninitiated readers were expected to think it a tedious exercise in philology, which they would skim while searching for more interesting passages in the *Guide*. Esotericists would instead attend to the topics that Maimonides raised in order to illustrate his philological argument. The juxtaposition of topics conveyed the esoteric subtext.

> *To fill [malle]*. This is an equivocal term applied by people speaking the Hebrew language to a body's entering and filling up another body. Thus: *And she filled her pitcher; An omerful for each*. This usage is frequent. The term is likewise applied to the coming to an end and completion of a measurable period of time. Thus: *And her days were fulfilled; And forty days were fulfilled for him*. The term is also employed to signify the achievement of perfection in virtue and of the latter's ultimate end. Thus: *And full with the blessing of the Lord; Them hath He filled with wisdom of heart; He was filled with wisdom and understanding and skill*. In this sense it is said: *The whole earth is full of His glory;* the meaning of this verse being that the whole earth bears witness to His perfection, that is, indicates it. Similar is its dictum: *And the glory of the Lord filled the tabernacle*. Every *mention of filling* that you will find referring to God is used in this sense, and not in the sense of there being a body filling a place. However, if you wish to consider that the *glory of the Lord* is the created light that is designated as *glory* in every passage and that *filled the tabernacle*, there is no harm in it.[17]

In this passage Maimonides discussed four ways in which the verb *malle'* was used in the Hebrew Bible. The word referred to: (1) the physical filling of a body with another physical body, as for example, an omer of manna; (2) the completion of a measurable period of time; (3) the perfection of a divine blessing or divine gift of wisdom; and (4) the immanence of the divine glory on earth. These associations were not casual. An esoteric message was intended to be conveyed through the juxtaposition of the concepts of manna, filling, a finite period of time, a divine gift of wisdom, and a vision of glory.

It is also significant that Maimonides's quotation from Exod. 16:33 was inaccurate. The biblical text referred to "a full omer of manna" that was to be placed in the tabernacle, but Maimonides wrote "an omerful for each," implicitly, for each person who ate manna. Equally intentional were the associations with a finite period of time, inspiration with divine wisdom, and the vision of divine glory.

The *Guide*'s second reference to manna occurs in a discussion of divine trial, which Maimonides regarded as "one of the greatest difficulties of the Law."[18] The topic had already been addressed, as we have seen, by Saadia Gaon. Maimonides began by remarking that people generally suppose that God inflicts calamities on people who have not sinned in order to increase their future rewards. To refute the popular belief, he cited the biblical phrase, "A God of faithfulness and without iniquity," and concluded by affirming the rabbinic teaching: "There is no death without sin and no sufferings without transgression."[19]

Maimonides's discussion to this point can be adequately treated at face value. Maimonides, however, did not exclude the case of ecstatic death from the talmudic rule that every death is a consequence of sin, and Maimonides's further discussion pertained esoterically to ecstatic death in particular. Maimonides asserted that trials are heuristic. He wrote: "The notion of a *trial* consists as it were in a certain act being done, the purpose being not the accomplishment of that particular act, but the latter's being a model to be imitated and followed."[20] Following this general definition, Maimonides cited the case of Deut. 13:4, in which a false prophet functions as a trial. However, Maimonides's indirect citation of the biblical text changed it from a negative to a positive example. "If a man claiming prophecy arise and if you see his suggestions tend to make one believe in the truth of his claim, know that God wished to make known hereby to the religious communities the extent of your certitude with regard to His Law."[21]

Not only was the topic of death to be associated with the idea of a trial that involved genuine prophecy, but Maimonides went on to discuss three further instances in which the Hebrew Bible speaks of trials. All three pertained to manna.

> *That He might afflict thee, to try thee out, to know what was in thy heart, whether thou wouldest keep His commandments, or no.* The meaning of this is: in order that the religious communities should know this and that it should be generally accepted throughout the world that those who wholly devote themselves to His service, may He be exalted, are provided by Him with food in an unthought-of way. The same notion is expressed when *manna* is spoken of on the occasion when it first came down: *That I may try them out, whether they will walk in My Torah, or no;* which means: in order that everyone should consider this and should see whether being devoted to His service is useful and sufficient or not sufficient. As for what is said [in Scripture] for the third time again concerning *manna*— namely, *Who fed thee in the wilderness with manna, which thy fathers knew not, that He might afflict thee, and that He might try thee out [nasotekha], to do thee good at thy latter end . . .* this dictum [means] . . . in order that it should be known whether being devoted to God does or does not suffice as far as food is concerned and gives relief from fatigue and weariness.[22]

Further ideas were associated through Maimonides's discussion of two further instances of trials: the case of false prophecy, and the biblical story of Abraham's response to the command that he sacrifice Isaac.[23] The juxtaposition of the two topics implies that Abraham's commandment to sacrifice Isaac was to be treated as an instance of false prophecy. It was a genuinely spiritual experience that was somehow corrupted in a manner that made its apparent content false and unreliable. Maimonides discussed trials no further, because he was utilizing the esoteric literary technique that was called *rashei perakim,* "heads of chapters." The completion of his train of thought was left to his readers. We are presumably to infer that experiences of ecstatic death, induced by manna, are trials because they are further instances of false prophecy. People interpret the experiences incorrectly, and so are misled by their apparent meaning, when they maintain that suffering occurs in the absence of sin. The correct interpretation, Maimonides asserted, is that the experience is false and a consequence of sin. In this way, Maimonides categorically maintained the talmudic position: "There is no death without sin and no sufferings without transgression."[24]

Maimonides's teaching may be treated as polemic against Christian privileging of ecstatic death.

Rabbi Obadyah Maimonides

Late in Maimonides's life, religious revival movements devoted to *hasidut*, "pietism," arose in both Egypt and the Rhineland.[25] Both concepts of pietism were probably indebted to Bahya ibn Paquda's *al-Hidaya ila Fara'id al-Qulub*, "The Book of Direction to the Duties of the Heart," which blended rabbinic tradition with the ethics and ascesis of the early Sufis. Bahya's ideal of piety was ascetic but not mystical.[26] An instruction manual in love for God, his book mentions neither alternate states nor any meditation that can induce one. The Jewish pietist movements of the twelfth century both added mysticism to the ascesis. The Egyptian movement, which lasted into the fifteenth century, included Maimonides's son Abraham (1186–1237) and grandson Obadyah (1228–1265) among its early leaders.

In his *Treatise of the Pool*, Obadyah discussed manna immediately following a presentation of the standard theory of medieval Muslim and Jewish philosophers, that prophecy consists of a conjunction of the human intellect with a metaphysical Intellect that actively structures the sublunar world. Concerning manna, Obadyah wrote:

> Thou wilt be sustained with that with which thine ancestors were nourished in the wilderness, as it is said, "man did eat the bread of the mighty . . . and gave them of the corn of heaven" (Ps 78:25). Similarly it is stated "the heavens were opened"

(Ezek 1:1), "open to me the gates of righteousness, I will enter them and give thanks to the Lord. This is the gate of the Lord; the righteous shall enter it" (Ps 118:19). The generation in the wilderness attained perfection through the excellent master in their midst, who showed neither greed nor grudge in their instruction, imparting to each individual in accordance with his capacity of understanding. This is similar to the manner in which Reason itself proceedeth, "and when they did mete out with the omer, he that gathered much had nothing over and he that gathered little had no lack; they gathered each according to his eating" (Ex 16:18). Thus he proceeded, until they had mastered what they could of the Word of the Lord.[27]

Obadyah asserted that eating manna opens the gates of heaven, not only in the biblical past, but also in the experience of his contemporaries. His citation from Ezek. 1:1 alluded to the vision of the enthroned glory later in the same chapter and made explicit the connection of manna with visions of the enthroned glory. At the same time, Obadyah was concerned to promote a philosophical interpretation of the vision as an imaginative depiction, by means of images derived from the senses, of the angelic Intellect. Obadyah consequently stated that Moses had disseminated Reason, the Word of the Lord, precisely as manna was measured out. It was not only the enthroned glory, but the angelic Word, to which manna provided access.

EIGHT

Saint Bernard of Clairvaux

*T*he Cistercian order of the Roman Catholic Church was founded in 1098 as a reformation within the Benedictine order that sought to return to a stricter observance of the Benedictine Rule. The most important personality of the early Cistercian movement was Saint Bernard (1090–1153), abbot of Clairvaux, in France. Bernard was active in the western European politics of church and state from 1130 onward. In 1145, he succeeded to place a pupil on the papal throne and incite Western Christendom to wage the Second Crusade (1145–49). Bernard's beginnings were equally auspicious. At the age of twenty in 1110, Bernard, then a minor Burgundian aristocrat of Fontaine-les-Dijon, persuaded his brothers, cousins, and friends, together with one uncle— about thirty adults in all—to apply together as novices to the abbey of Citeaux. In 1115, Bernard was made abbot and sent to found the third Cistercian community, the abbey of Clairvaux in Champagne. Clairvaux founded its first daughter-house, Trois-Fontaines, only three years later. At his death in 1153, Bernard was the father of seventy communities, which, in their turn, had engendered another ninety-four—comprising half the Cistercian order.[1] His enduring importance to Roman Catholic Christianity led not only to his canonization, but also to his designation as "the last of the Fathers."

Our present concern is with Bernard's *Sermons on the Song of*

Songs,[2] which profoundly shaped the subsequent course of Western Christian spirituality. The *Sermons* provide an encyclopedic theology of the practice and experience of the spiritual marriage, in the literary form of an allegorical commentary on the Song of Songs. Bernard explained the lovers in the Song of Songs as God and the human soul, united in mystical communion.

In the present context, it is significant that Bernard began the very first of his *Sermons* with a series of allusions to the Eucharist. Among them was a discussion of Solomon's bread. "Be ready then to feed on bread rather than milk. Solomon has bread to give that is splendid and delicious, the bread of that book called the Song of Songs. Let us bring it forth then if you please, and break it."[3]

If we take Bernard at his word, he is telling us that Solomon had a bread that we too can eat. It is a bread that is associated with his Song of Songs. And because the Song of Songs, according to Bernard, is concerned with mystical experiences, Solomon's bread must similarly be associated with the spiritual marriage.

Alternatively, if we instead treat the breaking of Solomon's bread as a metaphor that signifies the exegesis of the Song of Songs, the motif transforms the whole of Bernard's *Sermons on the Song of Songs* into a commentary on a Eucharist that was already being practiced at Solomon's temple, centuries prior to Jesus. Because the *Sermons* present Bernard's teachings about mystical experiences, either interpretation—literal or metaphoric—associates an Israelite forerunner of the Christian Eucharist with mystical experiences.

Whichever way the trope of Solomon's bread is interpreted, there is no avoiding the conclusion that Bernard was privy to the mystery of manna. He knew of a bread that had had use as a mystical sacrament in the temple of Solomon.

How did Bernard come by his knowledge of manna?

A passage in the fifty-second Sermon tends to indicate that Bernard was familiar with internal controversies within the Syriac mystical tradition. By the late seventh century, Syrian mystics had developed alternative techniques for the performance of the Mystery of the Cross. Dadisho Katraya advocated a solitary practice of visualization as the means to achieve ecstatic death. The mental images consisted of the crucifixions of self as Christ crucified on a cross, with one's good or guardian angel crucified on a cross to one's right, and one's demon or evil angel crucified on a cross to one's left.[4] Isaac of Nineveh instead proposed a world-rejecting variation. He avoided the terrors of ecstatic death as unnecessary concessions to the body. In their place, he advocated the enactment of Jesus' crucifixion, baptism, and so forth, as actions of the disembodied soul in heaven, during deep states of trance.[5]

Bernard addressed these issues when, in his fifty-second sermon, his commentary arrived at Song of Songs 5:2, where the biblical text states, "I slept, but my heart was awake." Bernard rejected interpretations of the verse in terms of mortal death, natural sleep, and the death to spirituality that is a life spent in sin. He instead explained the sleep in terms consistent with the mystical theology of Isaac of Nineveh.

> It is a slumber which is vital and watchful, which enlightens the heart, drives away death, and communicates eternal life. For it is a genuine sleep that yet does not stupefy the mind but transports it. . . .
>
> The soul is drawn out of itself by a thought that is both powerful and holy, provided that it so separates itself and flies away from the mind that it transcends the normal manner and habit of thinking. . . . the ecstatic soul is cut off from awareness of life though not from life itself. . . . "O that I had wings like a dove! I would fly away and be at rest." . . . How good the death that does not take away life but makes it better; good in that the body does not perish but the soul is exalted.[6]

The sleep that is "the death of the just" consisted of a mystical vision of the soul's "transport," that is, of what is today called an out-of-body experience. During its transport, "the ecstatic soul is cut off from awareness of life," implicitly because it is in an anesthetized condition in a deep state of trance.[7]

The final sentence of this passage in sermon 52 remarks, "Men alone experience this."[8] Bernard immediately went on to discuss a different experience that he termed "the death of angels."

But, if I may say so, let me die the death of angels that, transcending the memory of things present, I may cast off not only the desire for what are corporeal and inferior but even their images, that I may enjoy pure conversation with those who bear the likeness of purity.

This kind of ecstasy, in my opinion, is alone or principally called contemplation. Not to be gripped during life by material desires is a mark of human virtue; but to gaze without the use of bodily likenesses is the sign of angelic purity. Each, however, is a divine gift, each is a going out of oneself, each a transcending of self, but in one one goes much farther than in the other ... you have not yet put yourself at a distance, unless you succeed in flying with purity of mind beyond the material images that press in from every side.[9]

Bernard here prioritized the ascension as it was outlined by Pseudo-Hierotheos. It begins with an ecstatic death and proceeds to a complete transcendence of images. Bernard termed it "the death of angels" presumably because he was indebted to a living tradition that had replaced Pseudo-Hierotheos's crucifixion of the mind, soul, and body with Dadisho Katriya's crucifixion of the self, its guardian angel, and its evil angel or demon.

Importantly, Bernard's allusion to "the death of angels" was inconsistent with his customary view of angels. In Bernard's view, angels were the "frequent and familiar guests" of a person who sought the spiritual marriage.[10] Angels attended and witnessed the communion of the soul and God. Angels also occasionally functioned as "go-betweens," bringing the soul and God together for their marriage.[11] They did so by manufacturing visual images. Bernard wrote:

I cannot see what this [Song of Songs 1:11] may mean if not the construction of certain spiritual images in order to bring the purest intuitions of divine wisdom before the eyes of the soul that contemplates, to enable it to perceive, as though puzzling reflections in a mirror, what it cannot possibly gaze on as yet face to face ... when the spirit is ravished out of itself and granted a vision of God that suddenly shines into the mind with the swiftness of a lightning-flash, immediately, but whence I know not, images of earthly things fill the imagination, either as an aid to understanding or to temper the intensity of the divine light. So well-adapted are they to the divinely illumined senses, that in their shadow the utterly pure and brilliant radiance of the truth is rendered more bearable to the mind and more capable of being communicated to others. My opinion is that they are formed in our imaginations by the inspirations of the holy angels, just as on the other hand there is no doubt that evil suggestions of an opposite nature are forced upon us by the bad angels.[12]

Bernard here specified "images of earthly things." Their alternative description as "spiritual images" pertained not to their contents but to their character as manifestations to "the eyes of the soul" or "the imagination." Angels also mediated visual images of both angels and Jesus in his "physical frailty."[13]

Bernard took for granted that angels were purely intelligible entities. In this doctrine, he stood within the learned tradition of Christian Neoplatonism, exemplified, for example, by Saint Augustine of Hippo and Pseudo-Dionysius the Areopagite. Bernard's doctrine of the angelic mediation of mystical visions was instead consistent with the views of many Muslim and Jewish philosophers and mystics of his period.[14] On the other hand, Bernard's concept of "the death of angels" instead echoes an earlier and less philosophical view that considered angels to be anthropomorphic. Although Bernard did not subscribe to the anthropomorphic view, he invoked it as a literary trope in order to allude to the angels of Pseudo-Hierotheos's sacrament.

To account for Saint Bernard's knowledge of the Syriac Mystery of the Cross, it suffices to assume that Syrian churchmen initiated crusaders in the Holy Land and the crusaders imported the initiatory tradition to western Europe.[15] Bernard was intimately involved with crusaders. Although Bernard declined the invitation of Baldwin II of Jerusalem to found a Cistercian monastery in the Holy City,[16] he helped to found the Order of the Poor Knights of Christ and the Temple of Solomon, who were more commonly known as the Knights Templar. According to Matthew Paris, writing in the thirteenth century, Hugh de Payens, the count of Champagne, along with eight companions, swore vows in 1118 to Patriarch Gormund of Jerusalem that they would be obedient, poor, and chaste, and that they would offer help and protection to pilgrims on the road from Jaffa to Jerusalem. Baldwin II granted them rooms in the royal palace, the so-called Templum Salomonis (now the mosque of al-Aqsa), from which the monks took their name. For help with the church in Europe, Hugh de Payens turned to Bernard, who was then prominent only locally but happened to be Hugh's relative.[17] Bernard drafted the "Rule of the Knights Templar," wrote *In Praise of the New Knighthood* as an apology for the knights, and secured the approval of the Templar rule at the Council of Troyes (in Champagne) in 1128.[18] Bernard later played a major role in the organization of the Second Crusade (1145–49). The pope who called for the crusade, Eugenius III (1145–53), had been a Cistercian monk at Clairvaux; and Bernard, who had earlier gained international stature for his role in ending the papal schism of 1130, intervened actively in European politics in order to keep control of the Second Crusade from passing from the Church to Louis VII of France.[19] At the very end of Bernard's life, the third master of the Templar Order, Evrard des Barres (1149–52), returned to France, left the order, and retired to Clairvaux where he took orders as a Cistercian monk.[20]

NINE

The Holy Grail

*J*n 1136, Geoffrey of Monmouth, a contemporary of Saint Bernard's, published *Historia Regum Britanniae,* "History of the Kings of Britain," retelling for an international audience the Welsh legend of King Arthur.[1] Historically, Arthur may have lived in the fifth or early sixth century and led the British resistance to invading Saxons.[2] In the 1170s, Chrétien de Troyes penned the first romances concerning knights at Arthur's court. Unfinished at Chrétien's death in 1180 was his *Li Conte del Graal,* "The Story of the Grail," the first written tale ever to mention the Holy Grail.[3] The Grail quest was retold several times over the next fifty years before the medieval vogue of the Matter of Britain began to pass.[4]

Different versions of the Grail quest identify the Grail differently. Etymologically, the term *graal* denoted a large platter, on which might be placed "pike, lampreys, and salmon"—to use Chrétien's phrase.[5] Chrétien, however, portrayed such a platter as bearing a single Eucharist wafer as its sole content. Robert de Boron introduced the idea that the Grail was the chalice that Jesus used at the Last Supper. The *Perlesvaus* described the Grail as appearing as five different objects. The Galahad quest made it a repository for Eucharist wafers. The *Parzival* of Wolfram von Eschenbach described it as a luminous stone.

To account for these and other features of the romances, Roger

Sherman Loomis reconstructed the oral prehistory of the Grail legends as follows.

> Their ultimate sources lay in Irish sagas, recounting the visits of mortal heroes to the palaces of pagan gods, where they were feasted sumptuously from vessels of plenty. Combined with other narrative patterns, these sagas passed on to the Welsh and left their traces in the *Mabinogion;* the original characters were replaced, the gods were euhemerized, and their dwellings localized. The deliverance of a Waste Land through the healing of its wounded king became a principal theme; a platter and a drinking horn became the principal sources of supply. This . . . material [was] transmitted orally through the Bretons to the French and Anglo-Normans.[6]

Welsh legend knew a platter of Rhydderch that instantly provided whatever food one wished.[7] It also knew a horn of Bran that had the same providential properties.[8] The two motifs were functionally equivalent. A tale that referred to the platter might achieve the same effect by speaking instead of the drinking horn. When the tale was retold in Christian form, both motifs persisted. Sometimes the Grail was a platter, but sometimes a cup.

To the all-important question why the Grail was associated with the Eucharist, there have been several theories but no firm answers. Arthur Machen noted that several of the romances portray heterodox rites of communion and speculated that the romances preserve a legend of the lost communion practices of the Celtic Church.[9] Alfred Nutt noted that Wolfram's *Parzival* identified the keepers of the Grail Castle as "Templesiens" and suggested that the heterodox rite reflected the historical practices of the Order of the Poor Knights of Jesus and the Temple of Solomon.[10] These and other theories continue to have their defenders."[11] Here, I would like to approach the problem more empirically.

Passover Allusions

Rabbinic midrash maintained that manna had whatever taste one preferred. Saint Basil of Caesarea (c. 329–379) cited Philo as his source of the Jewish tradition, and Saint Augustine of Hippo mentioned the motif as well.[12] Was it an accident that Breton *conteurs* selected the corresponding motifs of Celtic folklore for association with a heterodox version of the Eucharist?

Eugene J. Weinraub noted that Chrétien de Troyes described the meal, during which the Grail was displayed, in terms appropriate to the ritual meal, called a *seder,* "order," that Jewish families have celebrated at Passover since late antiquity. The Fisher King reclines on his elbow as Jews do at a seder. A young girl bears the Grail platter as, among Sephardic Jews, a young girl removes the ceremonial seder plate. Perceval fails to ask an expected question. In Jewish custom, four ritual questions are asked by the youngest boy present; in Sephardic practice, the boy additionally asks the girl who removes the plate where she is going and why she is removing the plate. The bleeding lance of the Grail procession compares with the Jewish custom of dipping a knife in wine, so that the wine may drip down onto the table or a plate, in memory of the plague of blood that God visited upon the Egyptians. Candelabras were used at the Grail meal, as also at the seder. Immediately before eating, the people assembled for the Grail washed their hands at table, as is ritually required at the seder. Tablecloths were used at both tables. In Chrétien, the meal consists of a *gastel* cake, meat, and a condiment, corresponding to the Jewish ritual obligation to eat *matzah,* "unleavened bread," lamb in commemoration of the Passover sacrifice, and bitter herbs. Not only does Chrétien's description of the *gastel* match medieval paintings of Jewish *matzah,* but the variant *gatey* was used to translate *matzah* into French in the glossary of Joseph ben Simson (1240). Wine was served at both meals. The repeated appearance of the Grail during the course of the meal compares with the repeated uncovering of the seder plate, which contains *matzah,* at specific ritual moments during the seder. The exotic fruits at the Grail meal compare with the *haroset,* a blend of ground apple, dried fruit, nuts, wine, and cinnamon that forms part of the seder. Finally, at both meals no food was consumed after the final cups of wine.[13]

Chrétien's presentation of the Grail meal as a Passover seder was presumably intended to allude to the Last Supper, the Passover seder at which Jesus instituted the Eucharist.

Access to rabbinic midrash and Jewish Passover customs was available to Christians in twelfth-century Troyes. Writing in the generation between Rashi and Chrétien, Peter Abelard (1079–1142) advised students at the Paraclete, the monastery that he built near Troyes, to learn Hebrew, the better to understand the biblical text.[14] Ecumenical contacts must have existed. Rashi's Bible commentaries occasionally respond to the views of Christian commentators; and the Bible commentaries of Rashi's grandson, the Rashbam (Rabbi Shmuel ben Meir), who succeeded his grandfather as head of the rabbinic academy in Troyes, exhibit personal familiarity with the Latin Bible and some of its Latin commentaries.[15]

The Syriac Mystery of the Cross

Because of the complexity of the problems surrounding Arthurian literature, it must suffice here to remark that the Grail was portrayed in unmistakable terms of the Syriac Mystery of the Cross not in the *Conte del Graal* of Chrétien, but only a half century later. The version of the Grail story that is entitled *Queste del Saint Graal* was composed in approximately 1225 by an anonymous monk of Saint Bernard's Cistercian order.[16] Sometimes called the Galahad quest, the *Queste* forms part of the version of the Arthurian epic that scholars term the "Prose Lancelot" or "Vulgate Cycle." Among the innovative features of the *Queste* is its description of the sight of the Holy Grail not as a sense perception of a sacred relic, but as a visionary experience that is granted by divine grace.

> When they were all seated and the noise was hushed, there came a clap of thunder so loud and terrible that they thought the palace must fall. Suddenly the hall was lit by a sunbeam which shed a radiance through the palace seven times brighter than had been before. In this moment they were all illumined

as it might be by the grace of the Holy Ghost, and they began to look at one another, uncertain and perplexed. But not one of those present could utter a word, for all had been struck dumb, without respect of person. When they had sat a long while thus, unable to speak and gazing at one another like dumb animals, the Holy Grail appeared covered with a cloth of white samite; and yet no mortal hand was seen to bear it. It entered through the great door, and at once the palace was filled with fragrance as though all the spices of the earth had been spilled abroad. It circled the hall along the great tables and each place was furnished in its wake with the food its occupants desired. When all were served, the Holy Grail vanished, they knew not how nor whither. And those that had been mute regained the power of speech, and many gave thanks to Our Lord for the honour He had done them in filling them with the grace of the Holy Vessel.[17]

The knights see the Grail in a vision that has been granted them by the grace of the Holy Spirit. What they behold is a covering of white samite. The covering conceals an object that is not itself seen. The ambition to behold the Grail openly and plainly motivates the quest that follows.

I omit review of the knights' adventures and proceed immediately to the climactic vision of the Grail at the end of the *Queste*. The account of the vision begins with an allusion to Ezekiel's vision of the chariot-throne of the glory. "It seemed that a man came down from heaven garbed in a bishop's robes, and with a crozier in his hand and a mitre on his head; four angels bore him on a glorious throne, which they set down next to the table supporting the Holy Grail."[18]

In the first chapter of the Book of Ezekiel, four flying cherubim support the figure of a man on a throne, who is identified as the glory of Yahveh. Like Philo, Saadia, and Maimonides, the *Queste* apparently understood that the enthroned glory was not divine. The man proves to be Josephus, son of Joseph of Arimathea, the first bishop of Christendom, who died over three centuries previously. Concerning his appearance in concert with the Holy Grail, he remarks that the "same service I performed on earth I still discharge in heaven."[19]

From the sequel, we discover that the Holy Grail is used sacramentally in a variant of the Eucharist. The *Queste* next draws unmistakably on the motifs of the Syriac initiatory tradition.

> Next Josephus acted as though he were entering on the consecration of the mass. After pausing a moment quietly, he took from the Vessel a host made in the likeness of bread. As he raised it aloft there descended from above a figure like to a child, whose countenance glowed and blazed as bright as fire; and he entered into the bread, which quite distinctly took on human form before the eyes of those assembled there. When Josephus had stood for some while holding his burden up to view, he replaced it in the Holy Vessel.
> Having discharged the functions of a priest as it might be at the office of the mass.[20]

Josephus next tells the knights that they will receive the Eucharist from Jesus himself. Then he vanishes. "Then the companions, raising their eyes, saw the figure of a man appear from out of the Holy Vessel, unclothed, and bleeding from his hands and feet and side.[21] The knights each have a vision of Christ crucified, emerging from the Grail. Jesus speaks to the knights, telling them that they have earned "some part of my secrets and my mysteries." Then he administers the Eucharist. "Then he took the Holy Vessel in his hands, and going to Galahad, who knelt at his approach, he gave his Saviour to him. And Galahad, with both hands joined in homage, received with an overflowing heart. So too did the others, and to every one it seemed that the host placed on his tongue was made of bread."[22] In the vision, the crucified Christ administered the consecrated Host from the Grail vessel. Because communion effects a union with Christ, each knight who saw Christ crucified was implicitly envisioning himself as Christ crucified, precisely in keeping with the Syriac Mystery of the Cross.

The Celtic Contribution

We may grant that the knightly behavior depicted in medieval romance left much to be desired by Cistercian standards,[23] and that the *Queste del Saint Graal* is perhaps better read as a fun-filled adventure story than as a careful work of theology. A basic question about the Grail legend remains: Why was the biblical mystery of manna expressed in popular literature by recourse to folklore that derived from Celtic paganism? What had medieval Wales to teach that Christian mystery initiates thought appropriate to their concerns?

The search for Celtic antecedents of the Grail has noted not only the platter of Rhydderch and the horn of Bran, but also the different motif of a cauldron. The medieval Welsh tale entitled "Branwen, Daughter of Llyr" relates that several mythic heroes of Wales invaded Ireland to avenge indignities done to Branwen, sister of Bran the Blessed. Bran, who leads the invasion by carrying the Welsh fleet on his back while wading the Irish Sea, was later known in Arthurian romance as the Fisher King and Keeper of the Grail.[24] In the battle that follows the Welsh landing in Ireland, the Welsh discover that the Irish make use of a cauldron of rebirth.

> The Irish began to kindle a fire beneath the cauldron of rebirth. Corpses were thrown into the cauldron until it was full, and the next morning they rose up fighting as well as before, except they could not speak. But when Efnisien saw the corpses, and no room at all for the men of the Isle of the Mighty, he thought, "Dear God, alas! that I have caused this desolation of men of the Isle of the Mighty! And shame on me unless I find a way to deliver them from this."
>
> He hid himself, then, among the Irish corpses, and two bare-bottomed Irish came and threw him into the cauldron as an Irishman. He stretched himself out in the cauldron, then, until the cauldron broke in four pieces, and his heart as well. From that came such victory as the men of the Isle of the Mighty got.[25]

Arthur Edward Waite concluded "that the Druidic Mysteries, as we find them in Welsh Legends, are like other Initiations: the Candidate is passed through the experience of a Mystical Death and is brought back, as, for example, by the Cauldron of Bran or that of Ceridwen, to a new term of existence."[26] Anthropologists have confirmed the initiatory significance of the motif of a cauldron of rebirth. During their initiations, some Siberian shamans envision themselves being killed in a cauldron, from which they presently resurrect.[27] Interpreted in the context of pagan Ireland, the medieval Welsh tale asserts that the Irish had initiations of their own. Although Celtic folklore bears ample evidence of a pagan practice of shamanism,[28] the tale of "Branwen, Daughter of Llyr" likely portrays an initiation into a warrior's mystery, rather than an initiation into the healer's art. The Irish are known to have initiated warriors into a type of ritual and ecstatic violence that the Irish called *ferg*, "anger." Comparable states were sought by Norse berserkers, in the ancient German *Männerbünde*, and their Scythian and Iranian parallels.[29]

The Welsh tale relates that pagan initiates were unable to speak, possibly in the sense that they lacked the prophetic word of God. In the competition of religions that is the story's implicit concern, the Welsh were able to defeat the pagans only because a Welshman underwent an Irish initiation in whose course he experienced an ecstatic death.

Another medieval Welsh tale, "The Tale of Gwion Bach," describes a similar Welsh cauldron. A magician named Ceridwen had a son to whom she wished to bestow "the spirit of prophecy."

> After laboring long in her arts, she discovered that there was a way of achieving such knowledge by the special properties of the earth's herbs and by human effort and cunning. This was the method: Choose and gather certain kinds of the earth's herbs on certain days and hours, put them all in a cauldron of water, and set the cauldron on the fire. It had to be kindled continually in order to boil the cauldron day and night for a year and a day. In that time, she would see ultimately that three drops containing all the virtues of the multitude of herbs would spring forth; on whatever man those three drops fell, she would see that he would be extraordinarily learned in various arts and full of the spirit of prophecy. Furthermore, she would see that all the juice of those herbs except the three aforementioned drops would be as powerful a poison as there could be in the world, and that it would shatter the cauldron and spill the poison across the land.[30]

In this tale, the pagan association of the cauldron with visions of ecstatic death has been replaced by a folkloristic concern with prophecy. The Bible's prioritizing of prophecy, in preference to all other varieties of ecstatic experience and behavior, was endorsed by this Welsh tale. The concern with psychoactive plants is explicit: a special preparation of herbs fills a person with the spirit of prophecy. Three drops from the cauldron, alluding presumably to the Christian trinity, are uniquely beneficial. All else that the cauldron produces, that is, every pagan use of the psychoactives, is poisonous.

Cad Goddeu, "The Battle of the Trees," is an independent poem that was attributed to Taliesin, the apprentice who drinks Ceridwen's potion and acquires the gift of prophecy. The poem contains the following lines, which refer presumably to the potion: "from a drop was the warrior killed. Peoples were made, remade, and made-again."[31]

Here the motif of ecstatic death was preserved as an alternative to the inspiration of prophecy.

Scholars are divided in their opinions regarding the antiquity of these medieval materials. The manuscripts in which the tales are found postdate Arthurian romance; but the materials seem to derive from an earlier period when storytellers addressed audiences who were comfortable hearing of pagan heroes and did not as yet demand exclusively Christian ones. Although the storytellers knew the meanings of the motifs for pagan religion, they were not themselves pagan. They were responsible for euhemerizing the Celtic gods, transforming Bran, Branwen, and others into mortal heroes. They and their audiences were apparently untroubled by what, from a pagan perspective, would have seemed sacrilegious. Moreover, the storytellers, or, at least the storytellers whose tales have come down to us, were themselves privy to a version of the biblical mystery. They knew that ingestion of a plant induced an experience of ecstatic death that served as an initiation into the practice of prophecy.

In this connection, we may take up the problem of the visit to the Grail Castle. Myles Dillon collected and summarized a group of Irish sagas that narrate the visit of a mortal to the palace of a god or goddess.[32] Loomis drew attention to one of them, *The Prophetic Ecstasy of the Phantom (Baile in Scail).* Written before 1056, it shows significant parallels to Perceval's adventure at the Grail Castle: "a supernatural figure who invites the hero to his abode, arrives before him, and acts as host; the lavish provision of meat and drink; the damsel with a golden vessel; the question, 'Who shall be served with this vessel?' which cannot but raise echoes of the question Perceval was expected to ask; the vanishing of the host."[33] Considered not merely as a folkloristic tale type but as an account of a shamanic experience, the narrative compares closely with shamans' reports of their journeys to the homes of the gods, where they are feasted, promised game animals and crops, promised health in their communities, and so forth. As I have shown in my study of Inuit shamanism, there is a risk during these journeys to the gods of the vision developing into an experience of ecstatic death. In the Inuit versions, a bizarre and ugly woman attempts to make the visiting shaman laugh. Should she succeed, she will immediately disembowel him. Should she fail, the shaman moves on to behold the lovely goddess of the sun.[34] In the Irish tale, the wife of the god Lug transforms "from extreme ugliness to radiant beauty"; the character persists in Chrétien's *Conte del Graal* as both the Loathly Damsel and the Grail bearer.[35]

In Inuit shamanism, a shamanic initiand will typically die and resurrect. It is only a much practiced shaman who will risk an ecstatic death but succeed instead to visit the gods in their home.[36] A similar pattern occurs in Celtic folklore, where the cauldron appears in initiatory contexts, but the platter and the horn in postinitiatory visits to the gods. Celtic storytellers were likely familiar with the relation of the motifs in a shamanic context. The cauldron and the platter were not interchangeable. The one was appropriate to a novice, the other to an adept.

When the motifs were developed into the Grail story, the

plurality of sacred vessels was reduced to one, in reflection of the unity of the Eucharist. The Grail was portrayed as a platter or a cup (or otherwise), but its meaning absorbed the significance that the cauldron had had in Celtic tales. The prioritizing of the post-initiatory pattern agreed the more closely with Judeo-Christian traditions that were publicly available. In many Jewish and Christian apocalypses, visionaries journeyed into heaven in order to visit the enthroned glory. The general public was unaware that Jewish *merkavah* mystics risked ecstatic deaths at the hands of angels who guarded the divine palace; while Syriac monks sought ecstatic death by way of preface to their ascensions to heaven.

The problem of dating remains. To account for Celtic story-tellers' knowledge of the shamanic meaning of shamanic symbolism, we do not need to go back to the pagan Celtic past. Danish Viking conquests in Ireland resulted in occasional alliances with different Welsh princes in the ninth, tenth, and eleventh centuries.[37] In the late eleventh century, Gruffydd ap Cynan (d. 1137) and Rhys ap Tewdwr (d. 1093), the legitimate rulers of north and southwest Wales, both spent time in Ireland.[38] Gruffydd ap Cynan was born in Ireland, the son of the daughter of the Danish king of Dublin. Following Gruffydd's return to Wales in 1081, court poetry underwent a revival that lasted through the thirteenth century. Tradition maintains that Gruffydd was accompanied both in exile and upon his return by poets and musicians.[39]

The literary connections of Rhys ap Tewdwr are more complex. On the basis of legal terminology and institutions, the *Mabinogi*, including the tale of "Branwen, Daughter of Llyr," has been dated to the period after 1050 and before 1120.[40] The prominence of Dyfed in the tales suggests their composition in south Wales,[41] possibly at the court of Rhys ap Tewdwr. Rhys was in Normandy under the protection of Duke William from 1055 until 1077, when he returned to Wales. Some influence on Welsh storytelling may be assumed on the part of the minstrel who, according to William of Malmesbury writing about 1125, sang of Roland to William's troops just before the battle of Hastings in

1066.[42] The *Chanson de Roland* is the oldest and greatest *chanson de geste*. With the help of William the Conqueror, Rhys established his kingdom in 1079; but in 1089 he fled to Ireland, assembled a fleet of Scottish and Irish seamen, returned to Wales and defeated the usurpers at the battle of Llychcrei.[43]

The Welsh invasion of Ireland in "Branwen, Daughter of Llyr" may echo the refuge taken in Ireland by one or both Welsh courts in the late eleventh century. The shapeshifting of Taliesin in "The Story of Gwion Bach" may have been indebted to the legend of the Irish poet, Amergin, rather than to continuous Welsh traditions.[44] It is not impossible that Welsh poets and storytellers, living among the Danes of Dublin, came into contact, if not with living practitioners of Nordic shamanism, at least with Danish storytellers who were familiar with the shamanic significance of common folklore motifs. Just as familiarity with Native American shamanism has led in recent decades to a renewed understanding of the shamanic significance of many motifs in Celtic folklore, so too in the twelfth century, contacts with Viking shamanism may have renewed Celtic understanding of folklore motifs whose meanings had been lost for centuries.

On the basis of these considerations, it is possible to argue that the biblical mystery was first celebrated in Welsh story early in the twelfth century, during the lives of Saint Bernard and Geoffrey of Monmouth. A half century later, the Welsh tales were worked up into Arthurian romance.

On the other hand, it is possible that oral antecedents of the Welsh tales are, as is commonly thought, much older. If the cauldron motif derives not from the Danish invasion of Ireland, but from an era when Celtic mysteries commanded popular devotion in Britain, we must think of a period well prior to the rise and spread of the Celtic Church in the fifth, sixth, and seventh centuries. We would then be obliged to postulate the historicity of a Welsh branch of the biblical mystery of manna during the Dark Ages that was originally independent of both the rabbinic and the Syriac branches. Indeed, it is intriguing to think that the pressure to compete with pagan Celtic mysteries may have contributed to the preservation of the biblical mystery in Britain.

Much historical research will be needed to firm up the hypothesis that a branch of the biblical mystery persisted in Britain from Roman times onward, as seems to have been Geoffrey of Monmouth's esoteric claim. If the hypothesis can be substantiated, it would suggest that Welsh initiates took the opportunity to bring their traditional esoterica to the attention of Roman Catholic authorities when, following the First Crusade, an independent branch of the biblical mystery was imported from Syria to France.

I have not as yet found what I regard as conclusive evidence that the biblical mystery was known in the British Isles prior to the eleventh century. I would like, however, to present three notable instances of strongly suggestive but finally inconclusive evidence. The character of Merlin in Arthurian legend was based on a fictional character in earlier Welsh poetry and folklore. A series of prophetic poems purport to be written by Myrddin, who went mad and commenced to prophesy following the battle of Arfederydd. The original nucleus of the poems may date from as early as the ninth century; most of the stanzas date after the beginning of the Norman invasion of Wales.[45] An early date is also suggested by the ascription of Myrddin's prophetic madness to his experience of battle. Although religious experiences are not typical symptoms of post-traumatic stress syndrome, they do occur spontaneously as symptoms of mania and acute schizophrenia. The Myrddin legend failed to distinguish among types of madness, but otherwise attempted realism. Notable by its absence from the legend was an understanding of the origin of the "mad prophet" tradition in the initiatory sickness of shamans.[46] The knowledge of shamanism in the Taliesin traditions was not expected of the audience of the Myrddin materials. *Ex hypothesi* the Danish impact on Welsh storytelling had not yet been felt.

The poem, "The Prophecy of Myrddin and Gwenddydd, His Sister," contains the following discussions of the Eucharist: "I will not take communion from cursed monks / with their pouches on their thighs; / God himself will communicate me."[47] The poem speaks of a divine communion, differing from the Roman Catholic Mass, to which a prophesying poet took recourse. Because the poem does not state that the poet's prophetic experience depended on his self-administration of the Eucharist, I treat it as inconclusive but supportive evidence of the historicity of a Welsh branch of the manna tradition. Importantly, the poem's hostility toward clergy on the grounds of their simony would be consistent with a date prior to a hypothetical rapprochement of Welsh esotericism with the Church of Rome under the auspices of Saint Bernard.

Another Myrddin poem, "Apple-trees," tells of the poet's estrangement from his sister Gwenddydd because he caused the deaths of her children.

> Sweet-apple tree which grows in a glade,
> Its peculiar power hides it from the men of Rhydderch;
> A crowd by its trunk, a host around it,
> It would be a treasure for them, brave men in their ranks.
> Now Gwenddydd loves me not and does not greet me
> —I am hated by Gwasawg, the supporter of Rhydderch—
> I have killed her son and her daughter.[48]

We may treat the sweet-apple tree as an allusion to the tree whose fruit Eve gave Adam to eat in Eden, according to medieval Christian biblical exegesis. The tree's invisibility to Myrddin's enemies would signify their ignorance of its correct botanical identity. The poem's statement that the tree "would be a treasure for them" was a straightforward assertion of the poet's faith. The immediate shift to the topic of the deaths of Gwenddydd's children implies that the deaths were ecstatic experiences. In other words, Myrddin initiated Gwenddydd's children into God's communion in a fashion that became public knowledge and resulted in his persecution by the king Rhydderch Hael, whom another Myrddin poem called "defender of the Faith."[49]

The last piece of evidence that I would like to review tends to indicate a period of better relations between the esoteric Welsh tradition and the Church. The hymn *Audite omnes*, "Hear Ye All," is the oldest Latin hymn extant that was composed in Ireland. Since about 800 C.E., it has been attributed to Saint Secundinus (d. 447), a contemporary and fellow missionary of Saint Patrick's, the Welshman who introduced Christianity to Ireland. The poem dates to Patrick's lifetime and was probably written in defense of Patrick during the controversy that followed his demand that the British prince Caroticus be excommunicated.[50] Of Patrick, the hymn states:

> Untiringly he feeds the faithful from the heavenly
>   banquet,
> Let those who are with Christ faint on the way;
> Like bread he gives to them the words of the Gospel,
> Which are multiplied like manna in his hands.[51]

In the context of the typical patristic references to manna, Secundinus's use of the motif is distinctive. Manna is not here an ancient and obsolete miracle. It is the food of a heavenly banquet that Patrick himself disseminates. It is a bread like the loaves that Jesus multiplied. At the same time, it is "the words of the Gospel." Does the text refer in this manner to Patrick's preaching of the gospel? Or was there an esoteric concern with Patrick's provision of ecstatic experiences of the divine Logos? The text is equivocal. Six stanzas later, Secundinus reverted to the topic of the Eucharist.

> A good and faithful shepherd of the flock won for the
>   Gospel,
> God has chosen him to watch over God's people
> And to feed with divine teaching His folk,
> For whom, following Christ's example, he gives his life.
>
> For his merits the Saviour has raised him to the dignity of a
>   bishop,
> That he may spur the clergy in their heavenly service,
> Providing them with heavenly rations, besides vestments—
> The rations of divine and sacred words.

He is the King's herald, inviting the faithful to the wedding.
He is richly clad in a wedding garment,
He drinks heavenly wine from heavenly cups
And gives God's people the spiritual cup to drink.

He finds a holy treasure in the Sacred Volume
And perceives the Saviour's divinity in His flesh.
It is a treasure he purchases with holy and perfect works.
ISRAEL his soul is called—"seeing God."[52]

Once again Secundinus mixed the motifs of feeding and conveying words. Patrick "feed[s] with divine teaching" and provides
"heavenly rations . . . The rations of divine and sacred words."
Once again, one must ask: does the text refer in this manner to
Patrick's preaching of the gospel? Or was there an esoteric concern with the biblical mystery, an eating of the psychedelic cata-
lyst of the prophetic experience of dialogue with God? The text
is ambiguous.

The last stanza that I have quoted makes more sense, however,
if we treat its second line in parallel with its fourth. "His flesh"
may be treated as a reference either to the flesh of Jesus, or to the
flesh of Patrick. The Latin is equivocal. If we interpret the line to
mean that Patrick "perceives the Saviour's divinity in his [Patrick's]
flesh," the final line of the verse ceases to be odd and becomes apt.
Philo's incorrect etymology of the name Israel as "seeing God"
was adopted, among others, by Eusebius, Jerome, and Augustine.[53]
Secundinus applied the phrase to Patrick in celebration of his many
famous dreams and visions. Patrick perceived the Saviour's divinity
in his flesh, that is, he saw God, in this life, while he was in the
body. Presumably, Patrick heard as well as saw.

TEN

The Kabbalah

$\mathcal{K}$*abbalah,* "tradition," was the name given to a distinctive school of Jewish mysticism that surfaced in southern France in the late twelfth century—in the very decades that Arthurian romance originated in northern France. Kabbalists called themselves *mekubalim,* "those who have received," that is, initiates. They wrote highly secretive texts that openly boasted of their possession of the secrets of the Bible.

The foundation work of the kabbalah, the anonymous *Sefer Ha-Bahir,* "Book of Brilliance" or "Book of Radiance,"[1] dates to the period 1170–1200. It introduced the kabbalah's system of ten *sefirot* (sing. *sefirah*), which are hypostases, or stages in the emanation of being. The *Bahir* introduced the names for the ten hypostases that subsequently became traditional in the kabbalah: (1) the Uppermost Crown (Keter 'Elyon), (2) Wisdom (Hokhmah), (3) Understanding (Binah), (4) Charity (Hesed), (5) Judgment (Din) or Strength (Gevurah), (6) Mercy (Rahamim), (7) Duration (Netsakh), (8) Splendor (Hod), (9) Righteous One (Tsaddik) or Foundation (Yesod), and (10) Presence (Shekhinah).

Although the kabbalah understands the *sefirot* as stages in the developmental origin of the cosmos, each objective condition of existence entails a distinctive subjective experience of being.[2] Rabbi Isaac the Blind, a late twelfth-century Kabbalist, explained: "Wondrous paths—these are the spiritual, inner essences. No being can contemplate them, save he who nurses therefrom. For (nursing) is a mode of contemplation *[derekh hitbonenut]* rather than cognition *[yediah]*."³ Thinking about the *sefirot* properly is to enter the alternate states that hypostases intrinsically are.

The ten *sefirot* comprise a typology of alternate psychic states that Kabbalists used as a map of mystical ascension toward God. The *Bahir*'s map of alternate states was as comprehensive as its author(s) could make it. In the *Bahir*'s system, the mystery of manna had an honored and important place. Kabbalists were urged to experience five different varieties of psychedelic experience.

Adverse Reactions

The *Bahir* consists of 141 paragraphs, each of which is a puzzle, written in code, whose subtext must be decoded in order for it to be understood. The topic of psychedelics first comes up in the course of three paragraphs that discuss adverse reactions to mystical experience.

> 27. His students asked [him]: What is [the vowel mark] *kholem*? He said to them: Soul—and its name is *kholem*. If you listen to her, your body will be vigorous *[khalam]* in the future to come. But if you rebel against her, there will return sickness *[kholeh]* on your head, and invalids *[kholim]* on her head. And they also said: that every dream *[khalom]* is in the *kholem*.

As part of its method of secrecy, the *Bahir* uses word plays in order to bring ideas into association. Reference to the vowel mark called a *kholem* permits the alternatives of healthy vigor *(khalam)* and sickness *(kholeh)* to be brought into association with dreaming *(khalom)* and the white jewel *(akhlamah)* in the dream. These associations intimate that dreams or, more generally, alternate states, may either be healthy or entail adverse reactions that are forms of sickness.

Like paragraph 27, paragraph 28 discusses a vowel mark.

> 28. He said to them: Go up and hear the grammar of the [vowel] dots of the instruction of Moses. He sat and interpreted for them: [The vowel mark] *khirek* hates the evil and punishes

them; and on its side are jealousy, and hatred and rivalry, as it is written, "He gnashes his teeth at them" [Ps. 37:12]. Do not read "gnashes" *[khorek]* but "distances" *[rokhek]*. Distance these attributes, and evil will distance from you; and all that is present in good will attach *[yiddebak]* to you. *Khirek*. Do not read *khirek* but "ice" *[kerakh]*. Every place where *khirek* attaches becomes ice, as it is said, "and it cleanses" [Exod. 34:7].

Reference to the vowel mark called *khirek* serves as a pretext to associate the sounds and ideas of two words that are spelled with the same three consonants: "gnashes" *(khorek)* and "distances" *(rokhek)*. The interpretation is then made that *khirek* punishes evil, causing the gnashing, but will also keep discomfort at a distance, if jealousy, hatred, and rivalry are avoided. In juxtaposition with paragraph 27, these ideas may be treated as a theory of adverse reactions. Adverse reactions are punitive consequences of jealousy, hatred, and rivalry. The association of *khirek* with ice *(kerakh)* is a pretext for intimating that the suffering of punishment serves the implicit purpose of cleansing.

Paragraph 29 appears, at first glance, to be unrelated to the preceding paragraphs. Using the circumlocution YYY for the divine name YHVH, the *Bahir* cites the seven occurrences of the expression, "voice of YHVH" in the biblical Book of Psalms as a basis for enumerating the seven lower *sefirot*.

29. Mar said: What of the scripture, "And all of the people saw the voices" [Exod. 20:18]? And only because the voices were seen, "all the people saw the voices." Of them King David said:

[1] As it is said, "The voice of YYY is on the waters, the god of glory thunders" and so forth [Ps. 29:3].

[2] "The voice of YYY with strength" [Ps. 29:4]. And it says, "With the strength of my hand I made it" [Isa. 10:13]. And it says, "Even My hand founded [Yesod] the earth" [Isa. 48:13].

[3] "The voice of YYY is with majesty" [Ps. 29:4]. And it says, "Splendor [Hod] and majesty are His labors, and His righteousness" [Ps. 111:3].

[4] "The voice of YYY breaks the cedars" [Ps. 29:5]. This is the bow that breaks the cypress trees and the cedar trees.

[5] "The voice of YYY draws out flames of fire" [Ps. 29:7].

This is what makes peace between water and fire. It draws out the power of the fire and prevents it from evaporating the water. It also prevents its flames.

[6] "The voice of YYY shakes the desert" [Ps. 29:8], as it is said, "He does kindness [Hesed] to his Anointed, to David and his descendants forever" [Ps. 18:51]—more than in the desert.

[7] "The voice of YYY makes hinds to calve, strips the forests bare, and in His Temple, one says 'Glory'" [Ps. 29:9]. And it is written, "I bind you with an oath, O daughters of Jerusalem, with the hosts, or with the hinds of the field" [Song of Songs 2:7].

This teaches us that with seven voices the Torah was given. In each of them the lord of the world was revealed to them, and they saw him. And this is as it is written, "And all the people saw the voice."

Three of the biblical verses that are quoted use, as ordinary words, terms that the *Bahir* secretly treated as names of the *sefirot*. The second voice is associated with the founding of the earth; and Yesod, "Foundation," was a traditional name of the second *sefirah* from the bottom. The third voice is associated with "splendor and majesty"; and Hod, "Splendor," was the traditional name of the third last *sefirah*. These matches suggest that paragraph 29 enumerated seven *sefirot* in the order of ascension. The seventh voice is consequently associated, among other concerns, with acute fear in response to the glory beheld in the Temple. In reaction to the voice of YYY, deer go into birth labor, forests are denuded, and people and angels render homage, saying "Glory!" The allusions pertain to panic attacks during visionary experiences. The Bahir implicitly alluded to the practice in the older system of *merkavah* mysticism, which envisioned ascensions to heaven and located the enthroned glory of God in the seventh of seven heavenly palaces.[4] Although *merkavah* mysticism located experiences of ecstatic death in the sixth heavenly palace, prior to the vision of the enthroned glory in the seventh, Saadia Gaon had identified the figure envisioned on the heavenly throne with the angel of death, and the *Bahir* here agreed with Saadia.[5]

Paragraph 29's citation of Song of Songs 2:7 associated Jewish women with both the angelic hosts of heaven and deer. The juxta-position of biblical verses implied that women, no differently than deer, may go into labor and suffer miscarriages in response to the voice of YYY. The association of visions of the enthroned glory with ecstatic death and spontaneous abortions suggests an awareness of the abortifacient pharmacological properties of ergot.

Ecstatic Death and the Tree of Eden

Another explicit reference to the experience of ecstatic death occurs in the final paragraph of the *Bahir*.

> 141. His disciples asked: Tell us how this worked. He said to them: Samael the wicked made a bond with all the hosts on high against his Master. Because the Holy One, Blessed be He, said, "And let him exercise dominion over the fish of the sea and the birds of the sky" [Gen. 12:26]. He [Samael] said, "How can we cause him to sin and be exiled from before Him?" He descended [with] all his troops and sought a com-panion like him [or, like his death] on earth. And he found the serpent. It had the resemblance of a camel. He rode on it, and he went to the woman. He said to her, "Did God also say, 'From all the trees of the garden . . .'" [Gen. 3:1]? He said: I will ask more, and I will add in order that she will worsen. She said, "He did not deny us [anything] except 'the fruit of the tree of knowledge that is in the middle of the garden. God said, 'Do not eat from it and do not touch it, lest you die'" [Gen. 3:2]. And she added two things. She said, "from the fruit of the tree that is in the middle of the garden," and it was only said to them, "and from the tree" [Gen. 2:17]. And she said, "Do not touch it lest you die." What did Samael the wicked do? He went and touched the tree. And the tree was screaming and saying, "Wicked one, do not touch me!" As it is said, "Let not a foot of arrogance come down upon me," and so forth, "There the evildoers lie prostrate; they are thrust down, unable to rise" [Ps. 36:11–12]. He went and said to the woman, "Here, I touched the tree and I did not die. Even you can touch it and you will not die." The woman went and touched the tree, and she saw the Angel of Death approaching her. She said, "Woe is to me. Now I will die and the Holy One, Blessed be He, will make another woman and give her to

Adam. Rather, behold, I will cause him to eat with me. If we die, we two will die, and if we live, we two will live." So she took and ate from the fruit of the tree, and she [also] gave to her husband. Their eyes were opened and his teeth were set on edge. He said to her, "What is this that you have fed me? Just as my teeth were set on edge, so will the teeth of all creatures be set on edge." He sat down for him in true judgment, as it is said, "a righteous Judge" [Ps. 9:5]. He called to Adam. He said to him, "Why did you flee from Me?" He said to him, "'I heard Your voice in the garden' [Gen. 3:10]—and my bones trembled. 'And I was afraid because I was naked' [Gen. 3:10]. Because I was naked of works, because I was naked of commandments, because I was naked of deeds." As is said, "because I was naked, and I hid" [Gen. 3:10] What was Adam's clothing? It was a cuticle. When he ate from the fruit of the tree, this cuticle was removed from him. He saw himself naked, as it is said, "Who told you that you were naked?" [Gen. 3:11]. Adam said before the Holy One, Blessed be He, "Master of the world, when I was alone, did I ever sin before You? But the woman that You brought to me seduced me from your words." As it is said, "The woman that you gave with me" [Gen. 3:12]. The Holy One, Blessed be He, said to her, "Was it not enough that you sinned? Rather, you caused Adam to sin." She said before the Master of the world, "The serpent enticed me to sin before You." He brought the three of them, and decreed upon them a decree of judgment of nine curses and death. And he then cast the wicked Samael and his sect from His holy place in heaven. And He cut off the feet of the serpent and cursed it more than all of the beasts and all of the animals. And He decreed that it must shed its skin after seven years and in great sorrow.

The *Bahir* quoted paragraph 200 almost verbatim from *Pirke de Rabbi Eliezer*, an eighth-century midrash.[6] One novelty of the *Bahir* is its use of the narrative to provide a lesson in the reading of esoteric texts. Unlike the midrash, the *Bahir* noted that Eve told the serpent two things that God had not said to her. She claimed that the forbidden fruit belonged to the tree of knowledge in the middle of the garden, when God had spoken of the tree; and she claimed that touching the tree was prohibited on pain of death. Having made these errors of overinterpretation,

Eve gave the serpent the opportunity to challenge her by touching the tree.

When the serpent touched the tree, the latter screamed in
protest. Among its remarks was the claim: "There the evildoers
lie prostrate; they are thrust down, unable to rise" (Ps. 36:11–12).
Because the serpent has legs and is able to walk at this stage in the
tale, the quotation refers, I suggest, to hystero-epileptic psycho-
motor attacks that occur as adverse reactions to psychedelics.[7]

When Eve touched the tree, she underwent a different adverse
reaction. Adding a detail to the midrash, the *Bahir* states that Eve
beheld the Angel of Death and implicitly had an experience of
ecstatic death. Wishing Adam to share her experience, she gave
him to eat as well. At this juncture, Adam's teeth were set on edge.
The motif alludes to the "gnashing of teeth" in paragraph 28 of
the *Bahir*. This experience is explicitly called "true judgment" (*din
'emet*), alluding to the *sefirah* Din, "Judgment."

The "judgment of nine curses and death" consisted presumably of
the nine *sefirot* other than Din, which manifest through the experience of ecstatic death, which is to say, through "true judgment."

Manna

Although the *Bahir* never mentions the word *manna*, two paragraphs cite a biblical verse that discusses manna.

> 127. A parable. What does the matter resemble? A king who
> had an army, and he sent them food and bread for the multi-
> tude. They became lazy, and they did not eat it. They also did
> not protect it, so the bread spoiled and grew moldy. He came
> to inquire and to discover if they had what to eat. He found
> they had moldy bread, and he found them embarrassed to ask
> [him] for other bread. As though to say, "This we did not
> protect, and shall we ask for other?" The king also became
> angry. And he took the moldy bread and commanded about it
> that it be dried and fixed as much as possible. And he swore
> regarding these men, "I will not give them other bread until
> they eat all of this moldy bread." He sent it to them anew.
> What did they do? They said to distribute it. They distributed

it, and each one took his portion. The eager placed his portion
in the air, and protected it, and ate it [while it was] good. And
the other took it and ate what he ate with relish. And the rest
he set down, and he did not protect it because he despaired of
it. And it spoiled further and grew moldy and he could not eat
it at all. He remained starving until he died. He was held
responsible for the sin of his body: "Why did you kill yourself?
Was it not enough that you ruined the bread at the start? And
when I returned it to you fixed, and you distributed it, and you
ruined your portion, and you were too lazy to protect it. And
not only that, but you killed yourself." And he responded, "My
lord, what was I to do?" And he answered him, "You were to
protect it. And if you say that you were not able, you should
have watched your friends and neighbors that divided the
bread with you. And you would have seen their doings and
their protection, and you should have tried to protect as they
did." They also questioned him: "Why did you kill yourself?
Was it not enough that you ruined the bread? But you added
more and killed the matter of your body. And you shortened
your days, or caused it. And it was possible that a construction
from above might have issued from you, who would have saved
you and your damage, and others and their damages. Therefore your judgment [Din] will be increased on all sides." He
was confused and responded, "And what could I have done
once I had no bread? And with what could I have lived?" They
said to him: "If you had worked and exerted yourself in Torah,
you would not reply stupidly and insolently like this. From the
content of your reply, it is obvious that you have not worked or
exerted yourself in Torah. And is it not written in the Torah,
"For not by bread alone does man live, but from all that issues
from the mouth of YYY does man live" [Deut. 8:3]. You
should have inquired and probed and asked what is the thing
through which man shall live.

The discussion of Deut. 8:3 continues in the next paragraph of
the *Bahir*.

128. What of it, "issues from the mouth of YYY"? This says,
he shall live by Torah. Of it, "issues from the mouth of YYY."
From here they said, "A peasant cannot be a *hasid*." If a person
does not bestow charity *[Hesed]* on himself, how is it possible
[for him] to be called charitable? And even if he is charitable
with human beings, and he is a peasant, he is not called a *hasid*.

And how can one be charitable with his Maker? By studying Torah. That all who study Torah bestow charity on his Maker. As it is written, "He rides the heavens with your help" [Deut. 33:26]. Of it he says, "When you study Torah for its name's sake, then you help Me and I ride the heavens." Then, "His pride is in the clouds" [Deut. 33:26]. And what of "clouds"? Of it he says "in the room of rooms." As the Targum translates, "His word is in the Heaven of Heaven." Therefore, "not by bread alone does man live, but from all that issues from the mouth of YYY" [Deut. 8:3], that is, Torah that issues from the mouth of YYY by which man shall live. And the fool "answers insolently" [Prov. 18:23] that if you had learned Torah, you would not reply [insolently] as you replied. Therefore he is punished. And what is his punishment? I have already interpreted it.

The parable in paragraph 127 is not self-explanatory. How can the soldiers have prevented their deaths by studying Torah, if they had no food to sustain their bodies? Equally problematic is the assertion in paragraph 128 that the punishment for failing to study Torah has already been described. What happened to the soldiers was that they died and were reprimanded after death. Both puzzles may be solved if we interpret the paragraphs in terms of ecstatic death, rather than physical, bodily death. The parable illustrates the doctrine of paragraph 28 that adverse reactions are punishments for wrongdoing. The soldiers' punishments consisted of their ecstatic deaths and subsequent experiences of guilty recriminations.

The reference to bread mold agrees, I suggest, with the implication of paragraph 29 that the psychoactive substance associated with Din was ergot, the fungus popularly known as "rust" that grows on the grains of rye, wheat, barley, and other cereals. The same esoteric ideas are also conveyed through the quotation "man shall not live by bread alone," which refers in Deut. 8:3 to manna.

Concerning manna, paragraph 128 cites a Mishnaic saying, "A peasant cannot be a pious person *(hasid)*." By adducing the Mishnaic saying in connection with manna, the *Bahir* makes the esoteric point that manna is associated not only with Din, but also with Hesed. Hesed is the fourth *sefirah* in the order of declension, and the seventh *sefirah* in the order of ascension—that is, Hesed is where paragraph 27 located the enthroned glory.

Paragraph 128 interprets Deut. 8:3, "by all that issues from the mouth of YYY does man live," as instruction concerning the avoidance of adverse reactions. Study of the Torah, the *Bahir* implies, is necessary for the successful management of psychedelic experience. Reference was not made to ordinary biblical study, however, but to Torah in an esoteric sense that derived from the association in rabbinic aggadah of the primordial Torah with Wisdom in the Book of Proverbs.[8] For the *Bahir*, Hokhmah, Wisdom, was the name of the second *sefirah*. A Kabbalist had to ascend from Hesed to Hokhmah if he was to study Torah and so avoid ecstatic death at Din.

Moses Lifted His Hands

Paragraphs 92 through 95 explore the motif of Moses raising his rod in his hand during the battle with Amalek in Exodus 17. The *Bahir* associated Moses' action with Abraham's acts of feeding passersby, implying that the Mosaic narrative is an esoteric account of Moses dispensing manna.

> 92. R. Yohanan said: "What of the scripture, "And it was as Moses lifted his hand, and Israel prevailed, and as he rested it Amalek prevailed" [Exod. 17:11]? It teaches that the world exists because of the lifting of the hands. What is its meaning? Because of that power which was given to our patriarch Jacob, whose name is Israel. Abraham, Isaac, and Jacob were given powers, [one] to each one of them, and it was given to each of them according to the attribute that he exemplified. Abraham bestowed charity [Hesed] in the world, for he used to invite all the comers of the world and all the passersby on the roads, for food, and bestow charity, and go out to greet them, as it is written: "And he ran to greet them from the opening of the tent" [Gen. 18:2]. And more, "And they bowed [to the earth]," this was a bestowal of complete charity. And the Holy One, Blessed be He, attributed [endowed] him in his attribute, and gave him the attribute of Charity, as it is written: "You shall

give truth to Jacob and charity to Abraham which you swore
to our forefathers in ancient days" [Mic. 7:20]. What is "in
ancient days"? It teaches that if Abraham had not bestowed
[Charity] and merited the attribute of Charity, Jacob would
not have merited the attribute of Truth, for it was in the merit
that Abraham merited the attribute of Charity that Isaac
merited Fear, as it is written: "And Jacob swore by the Fear of
his father Isaac" [Gen. 31:53]. Is there a man who will swear
in this way in the faith of his father's fear? But at that point
Jacob had not yet been given power, so he swore by the power
that was given to his father, as it is said: "And Jacob swore by
the Fear of his father Isaac."

The term *middah,* "attribute," was used more commonly than
sefirah in the *Bahir* as a technical designation of the ten hypostases.
The attribute that was given to Abraham was Hesed, Charity.

Joseph Dan suggested that the attributes given Isaac and Jacob
were the fifth and sixth *sefirot,* Din and Rahamim.[9] Din, the locus
of ecstatic deaths and other adverse reactions, corresponds to the
Fear of Isaac.

93. And what is it? It is chaos *[tohu],* from which is the evil
that confuses *[ha-mathe]* people. And what of it? It is as it is
written of it: "And the fire of YYY fell and consumed the
sacrifice and the wood and the stones and the dust and the
water" [1 Kings 18:38], and it is written: "For YYY your God
is a consuming fire. He is a jealous God" [Deut. 4:24]. And
what is it, Charity? It is the Torah, as it is written: "Ho, everyone
who thirsts, come to the waters; and he who has no silver,
come" [Isa. 55:1] to Him "without silver and without price"
[Isa. 55:1]. And he will feed you Torah and teach you for you
already have merited this by the merit of Abraham who used
to bestow charity, and used to feed "without silver" and give
drinks of wine and milk "without price." [Is your knowledge
exhausted? Rather, say:] What of wine and milk? [What] is
the connection one to the other? Only, it teaches that wine, it is
Fear, and milk, it is Charity. And why did he mention wine at
the start? Because it is closer to us. Do wine and milk exhaust
your knowledge? Rather, [say:] the image of wine and milk.

The quotations from 1 Kings 18:38 and Deut. 4:24 identify the
Fear of Isaac with fire. Discussing the second and third *sefirot,*

Hokhmah and Binah, paragraph 9 of the *Bahir* asserted that "Michael, the prince to the right of the Holy One, Blessed be He, is water and hail, and Gabriel, the prince to the left of the Holy One, Blessed be He, is fire."

The implicit association of Din with Binah—fire with fire—is consistent with the association of Hesed (Charity) with Torah, that is, with Hokhmah. The *Bahir* enumerates only eight parts of the body: the head, hands, torso, legs, penis, and female genitals (paragraphs 55, 114, 116). The hands, however, each occupy two positions, lowered and raised. Paragraph 93 suggests that the hands are Hesed and Din when lowered, but Hokhmah and Binah when raised. The doubling of the hands is expressed also through the doubling of wine and milk as the images of wine and milk. According to paragraph 32, the seven lower *sefirot* are the locus of visions; the three upper *sefirot* are the locus of purely intellectual experiences.

> 32. One scripture says, "And all the people saw the voices and the torches" [Exod. 20:18]. . . . And what did they see? The seven voices of which David spoke. . . . And yet we have learned ten. . . . And of three, it is said, "A voice of words you heard, but you saw no picture, only a voice" [Deut. 4:12].

Consistent with the distinction between visions and abstract intellectual mysticism, Din and Hesed are the images of wine and milk; Binah and Hokhmah are wine and milk, without images. The lifting of hands, from the positions of Hesed and Din to the positions of Hokhmah and Binah, constitutes a shift from *sefirot* that can be envisioned to *sefirot* that are purely intelligible. All four are associated with the food bestowed by Abraham, that is, with psychedelic experiences.

A further implication of the motif of raising the hands is a comparison of Jacob with Israel. Although Jacob was renamed Israel in the Bible, the *Bahir* does not make the obvious connection, because it intends Israel differently.

> 94. And because of the merit of Abraham who merited the attribute of Charity, Isaac merited the attribute of Fear. And

inasmuch as Isaac merited the attribute of Fear, Jacob merited the attribute of Truth, which is the attribute of Peace. And the Holy One, Blessed be He, gave Jacob an attribute like his attribute. . . . This is why "[And it was as] Moses raised his hand, and Israel prevailed." It teaches that within the attribute that is called Israel is the Torah of truth. And what is it, Torah of truth? Something that teaches the truth of the worlds and whose activity is in thought [makhshavah], and which erects the ten sayings through which the world is erected, and it is one of them. And He created in man ten fingers on the hands to correspond to those ten. And when Moses raised his hands and intended [mitkaven] with the minimum of his heart's intention [kavvanah] to that attribute that is called Israel, and in which is the Torah of truth, he alluded with the ten fingers of his hands, that it erected the ten, and if it will not assist Israel, the ten sayings will no longer be established every day. Therefore, "And Israel prevailed. And when he rested his hand, Amalek prevailed" [Exod. 13:11]. And did Moses cause Amalek to win, as it is said, "When he rested his hands" [Exod. 13:11]? Only, it is forbidden for a man to pass three hours with his palms spread toward heaven.

In paragraph 93, where "Jacob had not yet been given power," the patriarch signified the sixth *sefirah*, Rahamim. In paragraph 94, however, after Moses raises his hands, it is the people Israel, not the patriarch of the same name, who signify "the Torah of truth." Although Torah ordinarily signifies the second hypostasis, Hokhmah, the Torah of truth here apparently designates the first hypostasis, "something that teaches the truth of the worlds and whose activity is in thought, and which erects the ten sayings through which the world is erected, and it is one of them." The inconsistency is explained, however, by the qualification, "that attribute that is called Israel, and in which is the Torah of truth." The *sefirah* called Israel differs from the Torah of truth, but contains it. The phrasing explains a fine point of Neoplatonic detail: every hypostasis both actualizes itself and contains all lower hypostases in potential. The first *sefirah* consequently contains the second in potential; indeed, it contains all ten.

The quotation from Mal. 2:6, "Torah of truth was in his mouth," may be treated as an allusion to the induction of a mystical experience through the ingestion of a psychoactive substance. Moses' act of raising his hands, however, also coincided with a practice of meditation. The phrase, "Moses . . . intended with the minimum of his heart's intention," twice uses the word-root *kaven*, "intend," that was a technical term for meditation.[10] Scholem explained:

> The expression *kawwanath ha-leb* ["heart's intention"] is taken from the Targum and the midrash and means concentration of the spirit; from the Book *Bahir* on it was used by the Kabbalists in the sense of "mystical meditation" on the sefiroth. It serves as the fundamental concept of their mysticism of prayer.[11]

The meditation on the *sefirah* "called Israel" that was to be performed during a psychedelic experience was to be achieved by means of "the minimum of his heart's intention," that is, by thinking of as minimal a topic as possible. The precise detail of thinking about the ineffable is outlined in the next paragraph of the *Bahir*.

> 95. His students asked him: To whom are the palms raised? He said to them: To the height of heaven. And whence is this? As it is written, "The deep *[tehom]* gives forth its voice, it lifts up its hand on high" [Hab. 3:10]. This teaches that there is no lifting of palms except to the height of the heaven. And when there are in Israel intellectual men and they know the secret of the glorified name and they raise their palms, they will be answered immediately, as it is said, "Then you will call, and YYY will answer" [Isa. 58:9]. If you call "then" *['az]*, YYY will answer immediately [lit. at hand]. And what of it, "then"? Rather, Fear. It teaches that there is no permission to call and pray to the *'alef* alone, but by means of the two letters that are attached to it, that sit first in the kingship. And with the *'alef,* they are three. And seven of the ten sayings remain, and they are *zayin*, as it is written, "Then sang Moses and the Israelites" [Exod. 15:1] as well.

The "height of heaven," to which the palms are raised, is presumably the first hypostasis at the top of the *sefirotic* structure. "Intellectual men" are said to engage in raising their palms in allusion to the pure intelligibility of the upper *sefirot*. The quotation from

Hab. 3:10, "The deep gives forth its voice," uses the word *tehom,* "deep," which is cognate with both *tohu,* "chaos," and *metahe,* "confuse." The juxtaposition of the quotation indicates that the raising of the palms begins at *tehom,* the *tohu* of Din, the chaos of an ecstatic death. It then proceeds as high as the first *sefirah,* which is designated by *'alef,* the first letter of the Hebrew alphabet. *'Alef,* however, cannot be reached on its own. It is invariably contemplated in connection with Hokhmah and Binah. During psychedelic experience, contemplation of the discrete ideas of Binah and the unified All-Being of Hokhmah leads to "something that teaches the truth of the worlds and whose activity is in thought." The recognition that the "worlds" or states of being, Binah and Hokhmah, are "in thought," discloses *makhshavah,* "thought" or "consciousness," as the first *sefirah.*

At the same time, "the secret of the glorified name" is the esoteric doctrine, found in *Sefer Yetsirah,* that the highest level of being is the name YHVH, an angelic intelligence that is not to be confused with the Creator whose name it is. Consciousness *(makhshavah),* no differently than Wisdom (Hokhmah) and Understanding (Binah), is something created. The *Bahir* terms it *'alef,* a letter of the Hebrew alphabet, in reference to its inherently linguistic nature. A mystical experience of "consciousness" is a linguistic event. It is an act of communication from the Creator, a revelation.

This same sequence of psychedelic experiences is implied by the statement that "Jacob swore by the Fear of his father Isaac" because "at that point Jacob had not yet been given power." The *Bahir* considered mystical experiences of Din to be preparatory for the pure "thought" of the first hypostasis. Importantly, the Christian Neoplatonic itinerary of the *Book of Hierotheos* similarly moved from ecstatic death to contemplative union with the One.

Attainment of the *'alef* is not, however, the final goal of the *Bahir's* psychedelic experiences. The itinerary of mystical ascension culminates in prophetic revelation. When Kabbalists proceed properly, "they will be answered immediately." The phrase involves a wordplay. The term *miyad*, "immediately," is an idiomatic expression whose literal sense is "from [the] hand." The answering experiences of revelations implicitly occur at the ontological level of being that was designated as the hand, rather than at *'alef*'s rank of being, which corresponded to the head. The answers presumably consists of differentiated thoughts in the verbal stream of consciousness that is Binah, the upraised left hand.

In this manner, the *Bahir* agreed with the authoritative rabbinic tradition represented by Saadia, Rashi, and Maimonides, that associated manna with the experience of biblical prophecy.

The Charity of Abraham

Abraham's acts of feeding passersby is also discussed more fully, in a passage whose subtext concerns the ascension from Hesed to Keter.

> 132. . . . And is it not said, "Because Abraham hearkened to My voice," and so forth [Gen. 26:5]? What of "My charge"? Thus spoke the attribute of Charity [Hesed]: All the days that Abraham was in the world, I did not need to do my work, for behold, Abraham stood there in my place, and he kept my charge. For this is my work: that I cause the world to merit. And even when people are guilty, I cause them to merit. I also return them and bring their hearts to do the will of their father. All this Abraham did, as it is written, "And he planted a tamarisk in Beersheba," and so forth [Gen. 21:33]. He would set out his bread and his water for all of the world who came by, and he would cause them to merit. And he spoke to their hearts and said, "Whom are you serving? Serve YYY, God of heaven and earth." And he would expound to them until they would return. And whence is it to us that he would cause even those who were guilty to merit? As it is said, "Shall I then conceal from Abraham what I am doing? And Abraham shall indeed be," and so forth [Gen. 18:17]. Rather, I will give him merit. Because I know that he will seek mercy for them and he will be meritous.". . . And what of "My Torahs" [Gen. 26:5]? Only, he knew and fulfilled even the instruction and debating taught on high.

The idea that Abraham so performed charity that the attribute of Hesed had no need to act independently provided the *Bahir* with the opportunity to state that by giving people water and bread, Abraham caused them to have merit. The *Bahir* goes on to explain that because Abraham both was meritorious and prayed for mercy for the beneficiaries of his charity, God responded by considering the guilty to be meritorious. Importantly, this achievement of merit, that is, this attainment of the *sefirah* Hesed, occurred *prior* to the preaching that induced the guilty to "return." The sinners did not repent first and earn merit afterward. By eating Abraham's water and bread, they merited first and repented afterward. The *Bahir* also makes a further point. The term "return" has both the manifest sense of repentance and the esoteric sense of a Neoplatonic epistrophe, a "reversion" of the Many into the One.[12] The ascension from Hesed to Keter depended on "the instruction and debating taught on high."

Scholem remarked that the association of *khirek* with fire in paragraph 28 depends on a wordplay in Arabic. "The word for 'burn' in Arabic (but neither in Hebrew nor Aramaic) is *haraqa*."[13] The wordplay suggests the passage's composition by a Jew who spoke Arabic. Similarly, the references in paragraph 132 to Abraham preaching "the name of YYY, God of the world," and "YYY, God of heaven and earth" imply an awareness of Muslim views of Abraham as a "friend of God" whose monotheism was not distinctly Jewish. Because the citation of "all the nations of the earth will be blessed through him" implies a concern with interfaith issues, it is also possible that the expression, "their Father who is in heaven," was selected for paragraph 132 because the formula is shared by Jews and Christians.

Conclusions

Professor Elliot R. Wolfson of New York University has advised me that kabbalistic literature contains a great many more references to manna. The example of the *Bahir* suggests, however, that references to manna that refer to psychedelics are apt to be visible portions of more complicated and extensive subtexts that cannot be understood without detailed analyses. Here it must suffice to conclude with a single passage from *Sefer Ha-Zohar,* the "Book of Splendor."

The *Zohar* claims to have been written by the second-century rabbi Simon bar Yochai; but modern scholarship attributes its authorship to the copyist and Kabbalist Moses de Leon, who first began to sell copies of the book in the 1280s. Early reports, stemming from de Leon's widow, state that he composed the work by means of automatic writing that he attributed to an angel.[14] Like the *Bahir,* the *Zohar* knew of the mystery of manna. The *Zohar* went further and publicly asserted that manna continues to be eaten by Kabbalists.

> Every day dew from the Holy Ancient One [the first *sefirah*] drops into the "Lesser Countenance" [the fourth through ninth *sefirot,* collectively] and all the holy apple-fields are blessed. It also descends to those below, and it provides spiritual food for the holy angels, to each rank according to its capacity of perception. It was this food of which the Israelites partook in the wilderness. "Each of them ate the food of celestial princes" *('abirim)* (Ps.. 58:26). Said R. Simeon: Even at this time there are those who partake of similar food, and that in a double measure [on Sabbath]. And who are they? Fellows of the mystic lore, who study the Torah day and night.[15]

For many centuries, Jews accorded *Sefer Ha-Zohar* a status that was equivalent in authority to the Bible and Babylonian Talmud. It remains the authoritative sourcebook of the kabbalah down to the present day.

Epilogue

$\mathcal{M}$anna was a matter of public knowledge in the time of Moses. In later centuries, it became a mystery of the priests and prophets of Solomon's temple. The mystery was publicly divulged in the era of Hezekiah, Isaiah, and the Priestly writer, but it was afterward secret once again. The biblical mystery was known to Philo, Jesus, and a number of other Jews of the first century. Jesus renewed the effort to give the sacrament to the general public. Public disinterest, however, combined with official persecution to keep manna a priestly mystery.

In the centuries after Jesus, knowledge of the secret persisted, apparently independently, as a mystery tradition in both rabbinic Judaism and the Syriac Christian Church. Inconclusive evidence suggests that it may also have been preserved independently in the Celtic Church. The rabbinic tradition reached western Europe in advance of the Syriac tradition. Following the First Crusade, the Syriac tradition was integrated with the Matter of Britain, and the rabbinic tradition of manna was integrated with a broad interest in alternate states by the kabbalah. The Celtic contribution to the mystery of the Grail remains to be clarified.

This study has been limited to demonstrating the historicity of the mystery of manna. To make my case, I have noted the repeated association of eating manna with the occurrence of a variety of religious ecstasies. Whenever possible I have also documented associated ritual activities and references or allusions to grain and/or bread mold. I have made occasional remarks in passing regarding the theological interpretations that were placed upon religious ecstasies by the different writers; however, no consistent nor sustained examination of the theology has been attempted. Neither have I presented the reader with the advice that may be gleaned from several writers regarding meditations and visualizations that can be used to facilitate the drug state's development into a doctrinally valid religious ecstasy.

Given the present social and political climate, I have chosen not to continue this history down to the present day. Let me instead remark that freedom of religion is an important principle of civilized political life. I have no hesitation in advocating the repeal of laws that institutionalize juridical persecution of the biblical mystery. Alone among biblical offerings, the bread of the presence is named *berit olam,* an "eternal covenant" or "perpetual obligation" (Lev. 24:8).

APPENDIX

The Belief-Legend

$\mathcal{M}$odern folklorists define legends as tales that (1) are believed true by their culture of origin; (2) have human protagonists, and (3) are set in times and places that are purported to be historical.[1] The Swedish folklorist Carl Gustav von Sydow proposed that *Sage*, "legends," be subdivided into two categories, which he termed memorates and fabulates. Memorates were accounts of personal religious experiences, and fabulates were what memorates became when they were retold by individuals who disbelieved in the tales.[2] For example, in modern Western culture, the sighting of a ghost may be believed true by its first narrator(s), but treated skeptically by others. In current terminology, we would instead state that a legend becomes a folktale when it ceases to be believed. The Finnish scholar Lauri Honko recognized, however, that von Sydow had noticed something worth preserving. Honko suggested that the term "memorate" be reserved for tales that are narrated in the first person, and he introduced the term "belief-legend" *(Glaubenssage)* to refer to the same tales when they continue to be believed true even though they are narrated in the third person.[3] So defined, belief-legends are a subset of legends that meet three additional criteria: (4) they are narrated in the third person; (5) their antagonists are numina; and (6) their narratives portray human encounters with numina.

These considerations have important consequences for biblical studies. The great body of biblical narratives that were formerly classified as *sage* may instead be recognized as belief-legends, a subclass of legend (and of *sage*) that has a distinctive theoretic significance.

We know from modern research on belief-legends that both autobiographical and biographical accounts of religious experiences frequently report the contents of the experiences without mentioning that the reports pertained to the contents of alternate psychic states. People do not always know when they have experienced an alternate psychic state, and people who do know do not always trouble to mention the fact.

Because people trust personal testimony more than hearsay, believers tend to retell memorates in memorate form when there is a risk of the tales' reception as fabulates.[4] For memorates to be retold in the form of belief-legends, belief in the tales must ordinarily be shared by the storytellers and their audiences. For this reason, belief-legends may safely be regarded as expressions of beliefs concerning religious experiences. Belief-legends function in living tradition as exemplars of religious experiences of their types. The tales furnish paradigms for the interpretations of religious experiences; people who have religious experiences will draw on their familiarity with belief-legends in order to comprehend their own experiences. Belief-legends also contribute traditional themes and motifs to the contents of peoples' religious experiences; the contributions proceed unconsciously when they do not additionally proceed consciously. Again, belief-legends frequently have pedagogical use as classic illustrations of religious experiences. The experiences that they portray are often deliberately emulated.

Belief-legends are concerned less with historical truth than with experiential truths of living religiosity. In the course of their transmission, belief-legends tend to undergo schematizing simplification through the omission of biographically accurate but idiosyncratic details that are irrelevant to the tales' functions as exemplars of their types of religious experience. The tales may also be expanded through the introduction of new materials. The additional motifs are frequently of mythic rather than legendary character.[5]

These several functions of belief-legends are well known as they have been adapted in the mixed oral and literary traditions of Western mysticism. Consider the place of Ezekiel 1–3 in the history of Jewish mysticism, the legend of Muhammad's night journey in the history of Sufism, New Testament spirituality in Protestant Pentacostalism, the Book of Revelation in the history of Christian apocalypticism, and so forth. Although a tale may be fixed in writing, its oral presentation in preaching regularly adapts and modernizes it. In some cases, for example, Muhammad's legend, a renovated variant may itself displace earlier written versions. In oral tradition, there are of course no literarily fixed variants and few constraints on revision.[6]

Belief-legends are a minor byway of research in folklore. Much of the discussion pertains to UFO reports. Where fieldwork allows single memorates to be traced into belief-legends, the tales are seen as vehicles for the transmission of folk beliefs.[7] In a few studies, however, the genre was found to have exceptional methodological importance for the history of religions, because textual narratives were identified as belief-legends in the absence of the antecedent memorates. Maarti Haavio used the procedure to solve a literary mystery in the study of the Finnish *Kalevala*. He demonstrated that the poems concerning Vainamoinen are variants of tales that concerned shamans in other cultures, and he concluded that the miraculous and magical exploits of the character are properly understood, not as the activities of a sorcerer or a god, but as the contents of shamans' ecstasies and séance performances.[8] Åke Hultkrantz supplemented a historico-geographical study of North American Indian versions of the Orpheus myth with a thoroughgoing explication of the religious meanings of the tales. He demonstrated that the differences among tribal variants of the tale consistently reflected differences in religious beliefs and practices. In particular, whether the protagonist was or was not able to bring a person back from the realm of the dead corresponded to the presence or absence of a local shamanic practice of retrieving souls that disease-causing spirits had stolen. The tale concerned shamans' ecstasies in some tribal variants, but eschatological doctrines in others.[9]

In my research on Inuit shamanism, I inverted the order of argumentation and used memorates and belief-legends to clarify obscurities of shamanic experience. The presence of narrative units in Inuit tales of shamanic initiations led me to discern discrete stages of the initiation process. I also found that a belief-legend's concern with a religious experience may be implicit rather than explicit. Some belief-legends—and even some auto-biographical memorates!—are told in equivocal fashions that can be interpreted as descriptions of miraculous, supernatural, magical, or otherwise impossible events. Shamans sometimes equivocate for purposes of esotericism. In other cases, the equivocation may be an accident of an attempt at brevity, or to avoid confusing youngsters in the audience, and so forth. Whatever may motivate the narrative convention, equivocal tales are nevertheless to be interpreted as tales of religious experiences.[10]

In principle, there is no obstacle to the application of these several research strategies to the biblical text. Indeed, some readers may be pleased to know that my approach to the biblical text has a precedent in rabbinic teaching. Rabbi Moses Maimonides made it a systematic principle of his biblical interpretation to treat theophanies and angelophanies as the contents of prophets' ecstasies.[11]

The hermeneutic assumption is a modest one, and its explanatory power is considerable. Although we may not trust the fabulous tales as historical evidence of legendary men, we may reasonably treat them as evidence of beliefs and doctrines about prophesying in eras contemporary with the productions of the extant tales.

Notes

Preface

1. Carl A. P. Ruck, "The Wild and the Cultivated: Wine in Euripides' *Bacchae*," in R. Gordon Wasson, Stella Kramrisch, Jonathan Ott, & Carl A. P. Ruck, *Persephone's Quest: Entheogens and the Origins of Religion* (New Haven: Yale University Press, 1986), p. 188.

Chapter 1: Manna and the Showbread

1. For a discussion of the source-critical problems, see Bruce J. Malina, *The Palestinian Manna Tradition: The Manna Tradition in the Palestinian Targums and Its Relationship to the New Testament Writings* (Leiden: E. J. Brill, 1968), pp. 1–18.

2. I have deleted verse 7b and the opening two words of verse 8, because 7b is duplicated almost verbatim at the end of verse 8. Arguably, sources are to be divided; however, the direct speech in verse 8 commences with a subordinate clause, lacks a main clause, and makes excellent sense when treated as subordinate to verse 7a. It suffices to postulate that verse 7b originated as a scribal error of duplication, which was subsequently "corrected" through an editor's insertion of "And Moses said" at the start of verse 8.

3. Richard Elliott Friedman, *Who Wrote the Bible?* (New York: Harper & Row), 1987, p. 210.

4. Tryggve N. D. Mettinger, *The Dethronement of Sabaoth: Studies in the Shem and Kabod Theologies* (Lund: CWK Gleerup, 1982).

5. Because manna was psychoactive, it is not possible to endorse its conventional botanical identifications with the gum of a desert tree, such as *Tamarix mannifera,* or a lichen of the *Lecanora* genus, or an excretion from an insect; on which see: Harold N. Moldenke & Alma L. Moldenke, *Plants of the Bible* (Waltham, Mass.: Chronica Botanica Company, 1952), pp. 125–28; R. A. Donkin, *Manna: An Historical Geography* (The Hague, Boston, & London: Dr. W. Junk B.V. Publishers, 1980). Neither is there evidence to support the cavalier allegation of John M. Allegro, *The Sacred Mushroom and the Cross: A Study of the Nature and Origins of Christianity within the Fertility Cults of the Ancient Near East* (1970; rpt. Don Mills, Ont.: PaperJacks/General Publishing Co., 1971), p. 112, that manna was *amanita muscaria,* the fly agaric mushroom.

6. Isa. 11:1–3 refers explicitly to the use of a psychoactive substance in connection with the practice of prophecy, but in a context that was not necessarily sacramental.

> (1)A shoot shall exit from the stump of Jesse,
> and a branch from his roots will bear fruit.
> (2)And He shall rest on him a breeze/spirit of Yahweh
> a breeze/spirit of wisdom and understanding
> a breeze/spirit of counsel and heroism
> a breeze/spirit of knowledge and fear of Yahweh.
> (3)And he will cause him to partake of the fragrance of the fear/
>   vision of Yahweh
> and he will not judge according to the vision of his eyes
> nor will he decide according to the hearing of his ears.

Isaiah's penchant for alliteration and double entendre is prominent in this passage. The word *ruah,* which occurs four times in verse 11:2, means both "breeze" or "wind" and "spirit." The cognitive character of wisdom, understanding, counsel, heroism, and knowledge indicate that Isaiah intended *ruah* in its sense as "spirit." In the first line of verse 3, however, he played by alliteration on the cognate word *reah,* "smell, scent, fragrance," which occurs in its verb form *heriho,* "he caused him to smell." In the same line, Isaiah also made use of the ambiguity of the word *yir'ah,* which may mean either "fear" or "vision." In the first occurrence of *yir'ah* in line 2d, where *yir'ah* is parallel with "knowledge," Isaiah almost certainly intended the reading "knowledge and fear of Yahweh." However, the reading of *yir'ah* in the next line (3a) is equivocal. Is it the fear or the vision of Yahweh that has a fragrance? Having read *yir'ah* in the sense of "fear" in 2d, we are presumably expected to read it in the same way in 3a, until we come to line 3b and encounter the cognate term *mar'eh*, which univocally means "vision." Having read *mar'eh* in 3b, we are presumably expected to revisit 3a and make sense of the verse by understanding *yir'ah* to mean "vision" rather than "fear." Isaiah's prophecy was that the shoot of Jesse would trust his vision of Yahweh, rather than the vision of his eyes. He would trust his spiritual experience over his sensory perceptions. Isaiah's concept of "the fragrance of the vision of Yahweh" presumably refers to a strong smelling psychoactive substance that was absorbed through inhalation, as for example, cannabis.

7. The many biblical passages that associate a miraculous provision of quails with manna, presumably alluded to sacrificial offerings of quail on the Passover.

8. The problem was noted by P. A. H. de Boer, "An Aspect of Sacrifice," in *Studies in the Religion of Ancient Israel: Supplements to Vetus Testamentum* (Leiden: E. J. Brill, 1972), pp. 27–30.

9. Menachen Haran, *Temples and Temple-Service in Ancient Israel: An Inquiry into the Character of Cult Phenomena and the Historical Setting of the Priestly School* (Oxford: Clarendon Press, 1978; rpt. Winona Lake, Ind.: Eisenbrauns, 1985), p. 210.

10. Most source divisions differentiate the "meal offering of jealousy" from the "meal offering of remembrance" in Num. 5:15, but then encounter major difficulties in verses 18, and 25 to 26. I have instead proceeded using different criteria. Because verses 24b and 27b duplicate each other, I omit verse 24b as an editorial link.

11. The juridical use of poison ordeals is widely known in Africa, Madagascar, and India; see: Sir James George Frazer, *Folk-Lore in the Old Testament: Studies in Comparative Religion, Legend and Law*, 3 vols. (London: Macmillan & Co., 1918), 3. 304–414; Theodor H. Gaster, *Myth, Legend, and Custom in the Old Testament: A Comparative Study with chapters from Sir James G. Frazer's Folklore in the Old Testament*, 2 vols. (1969; rpt. New York: Harper Torchbooks, 1975), 1, 280–300.

12. George Barger, *Ergot and Ergotism: A Monograph* (London: Gurney and Jackson, 1931); Frank James Bove, *The Story of Ergot* (Basel & New York: S. Karger, 1970).

13. Barger, *Ergot and Ergotism*, pp. 23–24.

14. Ibid., p. 21.

15. Ibid., pp. 30–31.

16. Working backward from the concluding reference to an innocent woman being able to conceive children (Num. 5:28), the New Revised Standard Version translates the symptoms more euphemistically as "her womb shall discharge, her uterus drop" (verse 27). Although ergot alkaloids are used medically to facilitate labor, Barger (pp. 178, 229) stated that they have proved experimentally to be unable to cause abortions. On the other hand, Richard Evans Schultes and Albert Hofmann, *Plants of the Gods: Origins of Hallucinogenic Use* (New York: McGraw-Hill, 1979), p. 103, asserted that "abortions of women were general during . . . attacks" of ergotism.

17. Brevard S. Childs, *The Book of Exodus: A Critical, Theological Commentary* (Philadelphia: Westminster Press, 1974), p. 268.

18. R. Gordon Wasson, Carl A. P. Ruck, and Albert Hofmann, *The Road to Eleusis: Unveiling the Secret of the Mysteries* (New York: Harcourt Brace Jovanovich, 1978), plate 9.

19. William Henry Propp, *Water in the Wilderness: A Biblical Motif and Its Mythological Background* (Atlanta, Ga.: Scholars Press, 1987), pp. 51–52.

20. Harold Henry Rowley, *From Joseph to Joshua: Biblical Traditions in the Light of Archaeology* (London: British Academy/Oxford University Press, 1950), p. 104.

21. G. R. Driver, "Two Problems in the Old Testament," *Syria* 33 (1956): 73–77.

22. Wasson, Ruck, and Hofmann, *Road to Eleusis*, p. 32.

23. Rabbinic tradition associated the Sinai theophany with experiences of initiatory death; the means of induction has not been established. See: Ira Chernus, *Mysticism in Rabbinic Judaism: Studies in the History of Midrash* (Berlin & New York: Walter de Gruyter, 1982).

24. See appendix, "The Belief-Legend," p. 147.

25. Verse 16b, which commands the gathering of an omer of manna, contradicts verse 16a and is presumably derived from a different source. Verse 18a is a further interpolation.

26. Jonathan Ott, *Pharmacotheon: Entheogenic Drugs, Their Plant Sources and History* (Kennewick, Wash.: Natural Products Co., 1993), pp. 139–40.

27. Useful studies include: Randolf Alnaes, "Therapeutic Application of the Change in Consciousness Produced by Psycholytica (LSD, Psilocybin, Etc.): The Psychedelic Experience in the Treatment of Neurosis," *Acta Psychiatrica Scandinavica,* Supplementum 180 (1964): 397–409; Sidney Cohen, "A Classification of LSD Complications," *Psychosomatica* 7 (1966): 182–86; Stanislav Grof, *Realms of the Human Unconscious: Observations from LSD Research* (New York: The Viking Press, 1975), p. 138-49; Dan Merkur, *The Ecstatic Imagination: Psychedelic Experiences and the Psychoanalysis of Self-Actualization* (Albany, N.Y.: State University of New York Press, 1998), p. 58–61.

28. Dan Merkur, *Mystical Moments and Unitive Thinking* (Albany, NY: State University of New York Press, 1999), pp. 87–93; Gershom G. Scholem, *Jewish Gnosticism, Merkavah Mysticism, and Talmudic Tradition,* 2nd ed. (New York: Jewish Theological Seminary of America, 1965), p. 15; Henry Corbin, *Avicenna and the Visionary Recital,* trans. Willard R. Trask (1954; rpt. Irving, Tex.: Spring Publications, 1980), pp. 156–57, idem, *The Man of Light in Iranian Sufism,* trans. Nancy Pearson (1971; rpt. Boulder, Colo.: Shambhala, 1978), p. 79; Mircea Eliade, *Rites and Symbols of Initiation: The Mysteries of Birth and Rebirth* (Originally titled *Birth and Rebirth*), trans. Willard R. Trask (1958; rpt. New York: Harper & Row, 1975).

29. G. C. Curtis and M. Zuckerman, "A Psychopathological Reaction Precipitated by Sensory Deprivation," *American Journal of Psychiatry* 125 (1968): 255–60; Marvin Zuckerman, "Reported Sensations and Hallucinations in Sensory Deprivation—Research Data Pertinent to Thirteen Hypotheses and a Reformulation," *Origins and Mechanisms of Hallucinations,* ed. Wolfram Keup (New York: Plenum Press, 1970), p. 141–44; Dan Merkur, *Gnosis: An Esoteric Tradition of Mystical Visions and Unions* (Albany, N.Y.: State University of New York Press, 1993), pp. 34–35.

30. Moshe Weinfeld, *Deuteronomy and the Deuteronomic School* (Oxford: Clarendon Press, 1972), pp. 247–48.

31. My source division of Judg. 6:11–24. In verses: 11, 12, 20, 21, 22, Gideon encounters an angel. In the middle of these references to an angel, Gideon is speaking rather suddenly with Yahweh (verses 14 and 16). In verse 17, Gideon asks for a sign that it is Yahweh who is speaking to him. In verse 22, he realizes, for the first time, that he had been speaking to an angel (cf. Judg. 13:16, 21). Once verses 14, 16, and 17 are deleted, the natural breaks in the narrative war-

rant the further deletions of verses 15 and 18. Verse 15 reads as a non sequitur when placed after verse 11, but reads credibly following verse 14. At the least, verse 18 would need an introduction, "And Gideon said" before it could be read after verse 11; but because it would then follow the angel's greeting, its request not to depart would be unwarranted. The request of verse 18 makes better sense as the sequel to the request for a sign in verse 17. In sum, we may separate verses 11 and 12 and 19 to 22 from verses 13 to 18. The latter does not constitute a self-contained narrative but may be treated as an editorial insertion.

32. Dan Merkur, "Prophetic Initiation in Israel and Judah," *The Psychoanalytic Study of Society,* vol. 12, eds. L. Bryce Boyer and Simon A. Grolnick (Hillsdale, N.J.: The Analytic Press, 1988), pp. 37–67; and "The Visionary Practices of Jewish Apocalyptists," *The Psychoanalytic Study of Society,* vol. 14, eds. L. Bryce Boyer and Simon A. Grolnick (Hillsdale, N.J.: The Analytic Press, 1989), p. 125.

33. Michael A. Fishbane, "Studies in Biblical Magic: Origins, Uses and Transformations of Terminology and Literary Form" (Ph.D. diss., Brandeis University, 1971), pp. 229–31.

34. Patrick D. Miller Jr., and J. M. Roberts, *The Hand of the Lord: A Reassessment of the "Ark Narrative" of 1 Samuel* (Baltimore: Johns Hopkins University Press, 1977).

35. In a study that attempted to extrapolate from Mesopotamian patterns to the biblical record, Alfred Haldar, *Associations of Cult Prophets Among the Ancient Semites* (Uppsala: Almqvist & Wiksells Boktryckeri AB, 1945), p. 1, suggested that the Assyrian tale of Enmeduranki's initiation as a *baru* priest by the gods probably "refers, not to the historical origin of the *baru* priesthood, but to the rites performed when priests were initiated." The initiation rites would then have involved visionary experiences that replicated Enmeduranki's ascension to heaven and audience with the gods; on Enmeduranki, see W. G. Lambert, "Enmeduranki and Related Matters," *Journal of Cuneiform Studies* 21 (1967): 126–38. Hepatoscopy, the inspections of the livers and entrails of sacrificial animals, was nevertheless the method of divination that was most commonly employed by *baru* priests; see Ivan Starr, *The Rituals of the Diviner,* Bibliotheca Mesopotamica, vol. 12 (Malibu: Undena Publications, 1983). It is not impossible that the *baru* priests, who were ordinarily nonecstatic diviners, required themselves to experience ecstasy, if only once for initiatory purposes. The pattern of an ecstatic initiation, followed by a lifetime of nonecstatic ritual behavior, may also

be found in native North American shamanism; see: Åke
Hultkrantz, "Spirit Lodge, a North American Shamanistic Seance,"
Studies in Shamanism, ed. Carl-Martin Edsman (Stockholm:
Almqvist & Wiksell, 1967); rpt. in Åke Hultkrantz, *Belief and Worship in Native North America*, ed. Christopher Vecsey (Syracuse:
University Press, 1981), p. 64.

36. Alan W. Jenks, *The Elohist and North Israelite Traditions* (Missoula:
University of Montana, 1977).

37. The oral incorporation of divine words was already a prominent
motif in the Yahwist version of the Moses legend, which derives
from Solomon's era in the tenth century. "Yahweh put a word in
Balaam's mouth, and said, 'Return to Balak, and thus you shall
speak'" (Num. 23:5; cf. 23:16). The Elohist narrative in Exod.
33:17–19, 34:5–8 implicitly presents a precedent in the life of
Moses for the initiation ritual. The initiation rite is also presupposed in the Deuteronomic prophecy of a prophet like Moses, of
whom Yahweh stated, "I will raise up for them a prophet like you
from among their brothers. I will put my words in his mouth, and
he will speak to them all that I command him" (Deut. 18:18).

38. Moshe Greenberg, Ezekiel 1–20: *A New Translation, with Introduction and Commentary* (Garden City, N.Y.: Doubleday, 1983).

Chapter 2: Knowledge of Good and Evil

1. Merkur, "The Visionary Practices of Jewish Apocalyptists," pp. 119–48.

2. Frank Moore Cross, *Canaanite Myth and Hebrew Epic: Essays in the
History of the Religion of Israel* (Cambridge: Harvard University
Press, 1973), pp. 15, 19, 31–34.

3. Walter A. Maier, III, *Aserah: Extrabiblical Evidence* (Atlanta, Ga.:
Scholars Press, 1986); Saul M. Olyan, *Asherah and the Cult of
Yahweh in Israel* (Atlanta, Ga.: Scholars Press, 1988); Baruch
Halpern, "The Baal (and the Asherah) in Seventh-Century Judah:
YHWH's Retainers Retired," *Konsequente Traditionsgeschichte*, OBO
126 (1993): 115–54; Tilde Binger, *Asherah: The Goddess in the Texts
from Ugarit, Israel and the Old Testament* (Sheffield, UK: Sheffield
Academic Press, 1997).

4. Edwin Oliver James, *The Tree of Life: An Archaeological Study*
(Leiden: E. J. Brill, 1966), pp. 17, 181.

5. William Foxwell Albright, *From the Stone Age to Christianity: Mono-*

theism and the Historical Process, 2nd ed. (Garden City, N.Y.: Doubleday Anchor Books, 1957); Karen Randolph Joines, *Serpent Symbolism in the Old Testament: A Linguistic, Archaeological, and Literary Study* (Haddonfield, N.J.: Haddonfield House, 1974).

6. Saul M. Olyan, personal communication, 1984.

7. Mircea Eliade, "The Yearning for Paradise in Primitive Traditions," in Henry A. Murray, ed., *Myth and Mythmaking* (1960; rpt. Boston: Beacon Press, 1968), p. 62.

8. Ibid.

9. Ibid., p. 66.

10. Mircea Eliade, "Shamanism," in Vergilius T. A. Ferm, ed., *Forgotten Religions (Including Some Living Primitive Religions)* (New York: Philosophical Library, 1950), p. 306.

11. A subjective idealist, Eliade, in "The Yearning for Paradise" (p. 62), wrote of "ontological mutation" in the state of man. Ecstatics undergo mystical transformations; their nonecstatic co-religionists do not.

12. Stephen A. Geller, *Parallelism in Early Biblical Poetry* (Missoula, Mont.: Scholars Press, 1979).

Chapter 3: Philo of Alexandria

1. For a survey of Philo's philosophy, see John Dillon, *The Middle Platonists: A Study of Platonism 80 B.C. to A.D. 220* (London: Gerald Duckworth & Company Limited, 1977), pp. 139–83.

2. "Philo Judaeus," *Encyclopaedia Judaica* (Jerusalem: Keter & New York: Macmillan, 1971), pp. 13, 409–15.

3. Nahum N. Glatzer, *Hillel the Elder: The Emergence of Classical Judaism,* 2nd ed. (1956; rpt. New York: Schocken Books Inc., 1966), pp. 26–27; "It was said of Hillel that he had not neglected any of the words of the Wise but had learned them all; he had studied all manners of speech, even the utterance of mountains, hills and valleys, the utterance of trees and plants, the utterance of beasts and animals, tales of spirits, popular stories and parables, everything he had learned." Babylonian Talmud, Soferim 16:9; trans. Glatzer, *Hillel the Elder,* p. 30.

4. Erwin Ramsdell Goodenough, *By Light, Light: The Mystic Gospel of Hellenistic Judaism* (New Haven, Conn.: Yale University Press, 1935;

rpt. Amsterdam: Philo Press, 1969); idem, "Literal Mystery in Hellenistic Judaism," *Quantulacumque: Studies Presented to Kirsopp Lake,*
eds. Robert P. Casey, Silva Lake, & Agnes K. Lake (London:
Christophers, 1937), pp. 227–41; idem, "New Light on Hellenistic
Judaism," *Journal of Bible and Religion* 5 (1937): 18–28.

5. Walter Burkert, *Ancient Mystery Cults* (Cambridge: Harvard University Press, 1987).

6. Marvin W. Meyer, ed., *The Ancient Mysteries: A Sourcebook. Sacred
Texts of the Mystery Religions of the Ancient Mediterranean World*
(San Francisco: Harper & Row, Publishers, 1987), p. 4.

7. Philo, "On the Cherubim, the Flaming Sword, and Cain the First
Man Created Out of Man (De Cherubim)," par. 42, 46, 60; *Philo,*
vol. 2, trans. F. H. Colson and G. H. Whitaker (Cambridge:
Harvard University Press; London: William Heinemann Ltd,
1929), pp. 35, 37, 139; idem, "On the Giants (De Gigantibus)," par.
54, in vol. 2, p. 473; idem, "On Flight and Finding (De Fuga et
Inventione)," *Philo: In Ten Volumes (and Two Supplementary Volumes),*
vol. 5, par. 85; trans. F. H. Colson and G. H. Whitaker (Cambridge: Harvard University Press; London: William Heinemann
Ltd, 1934), p. 55.

08. Philo, "On the Cherubim," par. 49, p. 37; "Concerning Noah's Work
as a Planter (De Plantatione)," par. 26, *Philo, in Ten Volumes,* vol. 3,
p. 225.

9. Philo, "Allegorical Interpetation of Genesis II, III (Legum
Allegoria)," book 3, par. 100; in *Philo,* vol. 1, trans. F. H. Colson
and G. H. Whitaker (Cambridge: Harvard University Press;
London:William Heinemann Ltd, 1929), p. 369; second passage
from Philo, *Questions and Answers on Exodus,* par. 51, trans. Ralph
Marcus (Cambridge: Harvard University Press; London: William
Heinemann Ltd, 1953), pp. 98–99.

10. Philo, "Every Good Man is Free (Quod Omnis Probus Liber Sit),"
par. 14, *Philo in Ten Volumes,* vol. 8, p. 19.

11. Philo, "On the Special Laws (De Specialibus Legibus)," book 1, par.
319, vol. 7, p. 285.

12. Arthur Darby Nock, "The Question of Jewish Mysteries" (1937);
rpt. in *Essays on Religion and the Ancient World: Selected and Edited,
with an Introduction, Bibliography of Nock's Writings, and Indexes,* ed.
Zeph Stewart (Oxford: Clarendon Press, 1972), vol. 1, 459–68.

13. Philo's access to the secret must at present remain a matter of conjecture. Gideon Bohak, *Joseph and Aseneth and the Jewish Temple in Heliopolis* (Atlanta, Ga.: Scholars Press, 1996), has argued, however, that the Hellenistic Jewish novel, *Joseph and Aseneth*, advertised the mystical practices of the Jewish Temple of Heliopolis. The novel refers to "the unspeakable mysteries of the Most High" (p. 7) among which, apparently, were experiences of death and resurrection that were associated with the motif of eating honey (p. 13). If Bohak's analysis is correct, the Jewish mystery that is discussed esoterically in *Joseph and Aseneth* may have derived from Solomon's temple. Around 170 B.C.E., Antiochus Epiphanes, the Seleucid monarch who ruled Judea from 174 to 164, replaced the high priest Onias III with two Hellenized Jews, named Jason and Menelaus. The actions of the latter soon led the Maccabees to revolt. In the meantime, Onias III, who descended from David's high priest Zadok, was murdered in Antioch, and his son Onias IV fled to Egypt, where he founded a Jewish Temple at Heliopolis. Assuming that the mystery of Solomon's temple was transmitted in the high priestly line of the house of Zadok as late as the period of Onias IV, it would have been preserved in Heliopolis; and *Joseph and Aseneth* may conceivably represent the Zadokite teaching. Other scholars, however, date *Joseph and Aseneth* to a period after Philo, in which case the Jewish mystery in the novel may have been derived from Philo, rather than vice versa.

14. Philo, "On the Cherubim," par. 62; p. 141; par. 60; p. 139.

15. Philo, "On Mating with the Preliminary Studies (De Congressu Quaerendae Eruditionis Gratia)," par. 167–74, *Philo*, vol. 4, 2nd ed., trans. F. H. Colson and G. H. Whitaker (Cambridge: Harvard University Press; London: William Heinemann Ltd, 1939), pp. 545–49.

16. Philo, "Who Is the Heir of Divine Things (Quis Rerum Divinarum Heres)," par. 191, *Philo*, vol. 4, p. 379.

17. Philo, "That the Worse Is Wont to Attack the Better (Quod Deterius Potiori Insidiari Soleat)," par. 118, *Philo*, vol. 2, p. 281.

18. Philo, "Allegorical Interpretation of Genesis II, III," book 3, par. 162, p. 409; see also par. 169, p. 415.

19. Philo, *Questions and Answers on Genesis*, par. 102, trans. Ralph Marcus (Cambridge and London: Harvard University Press, 1953), pp. 386–387.

20. Philo, "Allegorical Interpretation of Genesis II, III," book 2, par. 86, p. 279; see also: Ibid., book 3, par. 175, p. 419.

21. Philo, "That the Worse is Wont to Attack the Better," par. 118, p. 281.

22. Philo used the word *manna* only when he intended to convey an esoteric teaching. Philo nowhere used *manna* in "Moses (De Vita Mosis)," where he limited himself to the manifest sense of the Bible and discussed "the food which came from heaven" as bodily nourishment; see par. 200–210, 264–270, in *Philo*, vol. 6, trans. F. H. Colson (Cambridge: Harvard University Press; London: William Heinemann Ltd, 1935), pp. 379–85, 583–85.

23. Merkur, *Ecstatic Imagination*, pp. 91–101, 108–9, 145–48.

24. Philo, "Allegorical Interpretation of Genesis II, III," book 3, par. 175, pp. 419–21.

25. Philo, "On the Change of Names (de Mutatione Nominum)," par. 81, *Philo, in Ten Volumes* vol. 5, p. 183; idem, "On the Embassy to Gaius (The First Part of the Treatise on Virtues) (De Virtutibus Prima Pars, Quod Est de Legatione ad Gaium)," par. 4, in *The Embassy to Gaius*, vol. 10, trans. F. H. Colson, (Cambridge: Harvard University Press; London: William Heinemann Ltd., 1962), p. 5.

26. Philo, "On the Migration of Abraham (De Migratione Abrahami)," par. 201, in *Philo*, vol. 4, p. 249.

27. Philo, "On the Embassy to Gaius," par. 5, p. 5.

28. Philo, "Who Is the Heir of Divine Things," par. 78–79; p. 321.

29. On Philo's mysticism, see Andrew Louth, *The Origins of the Christian Mystical Tradition: From Plato to Denys* (Oxford: Clarendon Press, 1981), pp. 30–32; David Winston, "Introduction," in Philo of Alexandria, *The Contemplative Life, The Giants, and Selections*, trans. David Winston (New York: Paulist Press, 1981), pp. 21–34; idem, "Was Philo a Mystic?," in Joseph Dan and Frank Talmage, eds., *Studies in Jewish Mysticism: Proceedings of Regional Conferences Held at the University of California, Los Angeles and McGill University in April, 1978* (Cambridge: Association for Jewish Studies, 1982), pp. 15–41; idem, *Logos and Mystical Theology in Philo of Alexandria* (Cincinnati: Hebrew Union College Press, 1985), pp. 43–58.

30. Philo, "On the Change of Names (De Mutatione Nominum)," par. 258–60, p. 275.

31. Philo, "On the Birth of Abel and the Sacrifices Offered by Him and By His Brother Cain," par. 86; in *Philo*, vol. 2, pp. 159–61.

32. Philo, "Allegorical Interpretation of Genesis, II, III," par. 172–73, p. 417.

33. Ibid., par. 162, p. 409.

34. Ibid., par. 161, p. 409.

35. Philo, "On Flight and Finding," par. 137–39; pp. 83–85.

36. Walter Burkert, *Greek Religion* (Cambridge: Harvard University Press, 1985), p. 285.

Chapter 4: Manna and the Eucharist

1. R. T. France, *The Gospel According to Matthew: An Introduction and Commentary* (Leicester, England: Inter-Varsity Press; Grand Rapids, Mich.: William B. Eerdmans Publishing Company, 1985), p. 235; Jean Magne, *From Christianity to Gnosis and from Gnosis to Christianity: An Itinerary through the Texts to and from the Tree of Paradise*, trans. A. F. W. Armstrong (Atlanta, Ga.: Scholars Press, 1993), pp. 11, 15.

2. Paul J. Achtemeier, "Toward the Isolation of Pre-Markan Miracle Catenae," *Journal of Biblical Literature* 89 (1970): 265–91; idem, "The Origin and Function of the Pre-Markan Miracle Catenae, *Journal of Biblical Literature* 91 (1972): 198–221.

3. David Hill, *The Gospel of Matthew* (London: Oliphants, 1972), 255; France, *Matthew*, pp. 248–49.

4. France, *Matthew*, p. 237.

5. On Moses' miracle see J. H. Bernard, *A Critical and Exegetical Commentary on the Gospel According to St. John* (Edinburgh: T. & T. Clark, 1928), vol. 1, p. 175; Raymond E. Brown, *The Gospel According to John (i–xii): Introduction, Translation, and Notes* (Garden City, N.Y.: Doubleday & Co., 1966), p. 233. On Elisha's miracle see Bernard, *Commentary on the Gospel According to John*, vol. 1, pp. 177–78; C. K. Barrett, *The Gospel According to St. John: An Introduction with Commentary and Notes on the Greek Text* (London: SPCK, 1955), p. 279; J. N. Sanders, *A Commentary on the Gospel According to St John* (London: Adam & Charles Black, 1968), p. 178; Rudolf Schnackenburg, *The Gospel According to St. John* (New York: Seabury Press, 1980), pp. 15–16.

6. Bernard, *Commentary on the Gospel According to John*, vol. 1, pp.179–81; Brown, *Gospel According to John*, pp. 233–34, 247.

7. John Ruef, *Paul's First Letter to Corinth* (Harmondsworth, England: Penguin Books, 1971; rpt. London: SCM Press, 1977), pp. 89–90;

William F. Orr and James Arthur Walther, *I Corinthians: A New Translation, Introduction with a Study of the Life of Paul, Notes, and Commentary* (Garden City, N.Y.: Doubleday & Company, 1976), p. 247; Gordon D. Fee, *The First Epistle to the Corinthians* (Grand Rapids, Mich.: William B. Eerdmans Publishing Company, 1987), pp. 443–44.

8. Archibald Robertson and Alfred Plummer, *A Critical and Exegetical Commentary on the First Epistle of St Paul to the Corinthians*, 2nd ed. (Edinburgh: T. & T. Clark, 1911), p. 199; Fee, *First Epistle to the Corinthians*, p. 444.

9. Robertson and Plummer, *Commentary on the First Epistle of St Paul to the Corinthians*, p. 200; Orr and Walther, *I Corinthians*, p. 245; Fee, *First Epistle*, p. 447.

10. Malina, *Palestinian Manna Tradition*, p. 96.

11. Ernst Käsemann, "The Pauline Doctrine of the Lord's Supper," in *Essays on New Testament Themes*, trans. W. J. Montague (London: SCM Press, 1964), p. 113.

12. Jean Héring, *The Epistle to the Hebrews*, trans. A. W. Heathcote and P. J. Allcock (London: Epworth Press, 1970), p. 46.

13. Brooke Foss Westcott, *The Epistle to the Hebrews: The Greek Text with Notes and Essays*, 2nd ed. (London: Macmillan & Co., 1892), p. 149; F. F. Bruce, *The Epistle to the Hebrews: The English Text with Introduction, Exposition and Notes* (Grand Rapids, Mich.: William B. Eerdmans Publishing Co., 1964), pp. 120–21.

14. See, for example: Peter Borgen, *Bread from Heaven: An Exegetical Study of the Concept of Manna in the Gospel of John and the Writings of Philo* (Leiden: E. J. Brill, 1965); idem, *Logos Was the True Light, And Other Essays on the Gospel of John* (Trondheim, 1983); idem, *Paul Preaches Circumcision and Pleases Men, And Other Essays on Christian Origins* (Trondheim, 1983); Jean Daniélou, *Philon D'Alexandrie: Les temps et les destins* (Paris, 1958); L. K. K. Dey, *The Intermediary World and Patterns of Perfection in Philo and Hebrews* (Missoula, Mont.: Scholars Press, 1975); C. H. Dodd, *The Interpretation of the Fourth Gospel* (Cambridge: Cambridge University Press, 1953), pp. 54–73; R. H. Nash, "The Notion of Mediator in Alexandrian Judaism and the Epistle to the Hebrews," *Westminster Theological Journal* 40 (1977): 89–115; V. C. Pfitzner, *Paul and the Agon Motif: Traditional Athletic Imagery in the Pauline Literature* (Leiden: E. J. Brill, 1967), pp. 38–48; A. J. M. Wedderburn, "Philo's 'Heavenly Man'," *Novum Testamentum* 15 (1973): 301–26.

15. Magne, *From Christianity to Gnosis*, p. 42.

16. I. Howard Marshall, *The Gospel of Luke: A Commentary on the Greek Text* (Grand Rapids, Mich.: William B. Eerdmans Publishing Co., 1978), p. 898; Joseph A. Fitzmeyer, *The Gospel According to Luke (x–xxiv): Introduction, Translation, and Notes* (Garden City, N.Y.: Doubleday & Co., 1985), pp. 1555, 1559.

17. Alfred Plummer, *A Critical and Exegetical Commentary on the Gospel According to St. Luke*, 10th ed. (New York: Charles Scribner's Sons, 1914), p. 556.

18. Burton Scott Easton, *The Gospel According to St. Luke: A Critical and Exegetical Commentary* (Edinburgh: T. & T. Clark, 1926), p. 362; Eduard Schweizer, *The Good News According to Luke*, trans. David E. Green (London: SPCK, 1984), p. 372.

19. Easton, *Gospel According to St. Luke*, p. 44.

20. Brown, *Gospel According to John*, p. 101.

21. Euripides, *Bacchae*, 704–7, in *Euripides*, vol. 5, *Electra, The Phoenician Women, The Bacchae*, ed. David Greene and Richmond Lattimore (Chicago: University of Chicago Press, 1959), p. 185. Cf: Athenaeus 1.61 (34a); Pausanias 6.26. 1f.

22. Carl A. P. Ruck, "Solving the Eleusinian Mystery," in Wasson, Ruck, and Hofmann, *The Road to Eleusis*, p. 93.

23. Barrett, *Gospel According to St. John*, p. 157.

24. Philo, "Allegorical Interpretation of Genesis, II, III," Book III, par. 82, p. 355.

25. Merkur, *Ecstatic Imagination*, pp. 1-4.

26. Robert Tomson Fortna, *The Fourth Gospel and its Predecessor: From Narrative Source to Present Gospel.* Philadelphia: Fortress Press, 1988), p. 52; Leon Morris, *The Gospel According to John*, 2nd ed. (Grand Rapids, Mich.: William B. Eerdmans Publishing Co., 1995), p. 154, n 3.

27. Morton Smith, "On the Wine God in Palestine (Gen. 18, Jn. 2, and Achilles Tatius)," in *Salo Wittmayer Baron: Jubilee Volume* (Jerusalem: American Academy for Jewish Research; New York: Columbia University Press, 1974), English section, 2, pp. 815–29.

28. Fortna, *Fourth Gospel*, p. 53.

29. Philo, *Questions and Answers on Exodus*, 2, par. 45, pp. 89–90; 2, par. 47, pp. 92–94.

30. Alan F. Segal, *Paul the Convert: The Apostolate and Apostasy of Saul the Pharisee* (New Haven: Yale University Press, 1990), pp. 34–71.

31. Brown, *Gospel According to John*, p. 104–5.

32. Trans. B. M. Metzger, in James H. Charlesworth, ed., *The Old Testament Pseudepigrapha*, vol. 1, *Apocalyptic Literature and Testaments* (Garden City, N.Y.: Doubleday & Co., 1983), pp. 554–55.

33. Michael Edward Stone, *Fourth Ezra: A Commentary on the Book of Fourth Ezra* (Minneapolis: Fortress Press, 1990), p. 440.

34. Robert H. Mounce, *The Book of Revelation* (Grand Rapids, Mich.: William B. Eerdmans Publishing Co., 1977), p. 99.

35. R. H. Charles, *A Critical and Exegetical Commentary on The Revelation of St. John* (Edinburgh: T. & T. Clark, 1920), vol. 1, p. 65.

36. "2 (Syriac Apocalypse of) Baruch," trans. A. F. J. Klijn, in Charlesworth, ed., *Old Testament Pseudepigrapha*, vol. 1, p. 631.

37. Samuel Tobias Lachs, *A Rabbinic Commentary on the New Testament: The Gospels of Matthew, Mark and Luke* (Hoboken, N.J.: Ktav Publishing House; New York: Anti-Defamation League of B'Nai Brith, 1987), p. 153.

38. W. F. Albright and C. S. Mann, *Matthew: Introduction, Translation, and Notes* (Garden City, N.Y.: Doubleday & Co., 1971), p. 91; Francis Wright Beare, *The Gospel According to Matthew: Translation, Introduction and Commentary* (New York: Harper & Row, 1981), p. 204.

39. France, *Matthew*, p. 153.

40. Albright and Mann, *Matthew: Introduction, Translation, and Notes*, pp.149–50; Beare, *Gospel According to Matthew*, pp. 269–72.

41. Mekhilta Exodus 26:13. See also Mekhilta Exodus 31:14; Babylonian Talmud, Yoma 85b; Apocalypse of Baruch 14:18; Bablyonian Talmud, Erubim 43a.

42. Lachs, *Rabbinic Commentary*, p. 198. See also: F. W. Beare, "The Sabbath Was Made for Man?" *Journal of Biblical Literature* 79 (1960): 130–36.

43. Hill, *Gospel of Matthew*, p. 212; Jack Dean Kingsbury, *Matthew: Structure, Christology, Kingdom* (Philadelphia: Fortress Press, 1975), pp. 106–7; Beare, *Gospel According to Matthew*, pp. 269–72.

44. Herbert Basser, "Gospels and Rabbinic Literature," in Bruce D. Chilton, ed., *Finding the Missing Jesus* (Peabody, Mass.: Hendrickson Publishers, forthcoming).

45. Mishnah, *Shabbat* 7.2; Babylonian Talmud, *Shabbat* 73b.

46. Basser, "Gospels and Rabbinic Literature."

47. France, *Matthew*, p. 203.

48. Ibid., p. 225.

49. Albert, Hofmann, "A Challenging Question and My Answer," in Wasson, Ruck, and Hofmann, *Road to Eleusis*, pp. 33–34; Jane M. Renfrew, *Palaeoethnobotany: The Prehistoric Food Plants of the Near East and Europe* (New York: Columbia University Press, 1973), pp. 176–77.

50. Albright & Mann, *Matthew: Introduction, Translation, and Notes*, p. 185.

Chapter 5: Rabbinic Midrash

1. Shaye J. D. Cohen, "The Significance of Yavneh: Pharisees, Rabbis, and the End of Jewish Sectarianism," *Hebrew Union College Annual* 55 (1984): 27–53.

2. Stone, *Fourth Ezra*, pp. 31–33.

3. Scholem, *Jewish Gnosticism, Merkavah Mysticism, and Talmudic Tradition*; Ithamar Gruenwald, *Apocalyptic and Merkavah Mysticism* (Leiden: E. J. Brill, 1980); idem, *From Apocalypticism to Gnosticism: Studies in Apocalypticism, Merkavah Mysticism and Gnosticism* (Frankfurt am Main: Verlag Peter Lang, 1988).

4. Michael Edward Stone, "Lists of Revealed Things in the Apocalyptic Literature," in Frank Moore Cross, Werner E. Lemke, and Patrick D. Miller, Jr., eds., *Magnalia Dei, the Mighty Acts of God: Essays on the Bible and Archaeology in Memory of G. Ernest Wright* (Garden City, N.Y.: Doubleday & Co, 1976), pp. 414–52.

5. Louis Ginzberg, *The Legends of the Jews*, vol. 3, *Bible Times and Characters from the Exodus to the Death of Moses*, trans. Paul Radin (1911; rpt. Philadelphia: Jewish Publication Society of America, 1987), p. 44; texts cited: Tan. B. 2, 14 and 61 (text is corrupt); ShR 25.3; Yoma 75a; Sifre N., 89; Sifre Z., 197–98; Tosefta Sotah 4:3; Wisdom 16.21; Ephraem 1, 218. See also Josephus, *Antiquities*, 3, 1.6; *Recognitiones*, 1, 35; ER 12.60; BHM 6.39; vol. 3, p. 65.

6. Rashi, at Exod. 16:13; my translation.

7. Ginzberg, *Legends of the Jews*, vol. 3, p. 48; texts cited: Mekilta Wa-

Yassa' 6, 51b, and Mekilta RS 80.

8. Chernus, *Mysticism in Rabbinic Judaism*, pp.33–73 (see chap. 1, n. 323).

9. Ibid., p. 64.

10. Ibid.; texts cited: Tan. Sh'mot 25; Exod. R 5.9; Tan. B Sh'mot 22 (with some variations).

11. Ibid., p. 66.

12. Ibid.; texts cited: Lev. R 1.11; Song R 2.3.5. A variant occurs in the name of R. Joshua b. Levi in TB Yoma 72b.

13. Philo, "Allegorical Interpretation of Genesis II, III," book 2, par. 51, 56, 57; book 3, par. 29, 42–43; pp. 257, 258–59, 321, 329.

14. Michael Fishbane, *The Kiss of God: Spiritual and Mystical Death in Judaism* (Seattle: University of Washington Press, 1994), pp. 16–21.

Chapter 6: Pseudo-Hierotheos

1. Interestingly, Irenaeus read and quoted Philo; see P. Smulders, "A Quotation of Philo in Irenaeus," *Vigilae Christianae* 12 (1958): 154–56.

2. Irenaeus, *Adversus Haereses* 4.16.3; in *The Ante-Nicene Fathers*, vol. 1, *The Apostolic Fathers: Justin Martyr, Irenaeus* (rpt. Albany, Ore.: Sage Software, 1996), p. 994.

3. Irenaeus, *Adversus Haereses* 1.13.2–4, in Werner Foerster, *Gnosis: A Selection of Gnostic Texts*, vol. 1, *Patristic Evidence*, trans. R. McL. Wilson (Oxford: Clarendon Press, 1972), pp. 200–202.

4. Geo Widengren, "Researches in Syrian Mysticism: Mystical Experiences and Spiritual Exercises," *Numen* 8, no. 3 (1961): 161–98.

5. On the teachings attributed to Hierotheos by Pseudo-Dionysius, see I. P. Sheldon-Williams, "The ps.-Dionysius and the Holy Hierotheus," *Studia Patristica* 8 (1966), 108–17.

6. F. S. Marsh, ed. and trans., *The Book Which Is Called: The Book of the Holy Hierotheos, with Extracts from The Prolegomena and Commentary of Theodosios of Antioch and from The "Book of Excerpts" and Other Works of Gregory Bar-Hebraeus* (Oxford: Williams and Norgate, 1927).

7. Ibid., p. 232. See also A. L. Frothingham, Jr., *Stephen Bar Sudaili, the Syrian Mystic, and The Book of Hierotheos* (Leyden: E. J. Brill, 1886).

8. Marsh, *The Book of Hierotheos*, pp. 248–49.

9. Ibid., pp. 246–47.

10. Ibid., p. 28.

11. Pseudo-Dionysius, *The Complete Works*, trans. Colm Luibheid (New York & Mahwah, N.J.: Paulist Press, 1987), pp. 145–46.

12. Ibid., pp. 195–96.

13. Scholem, *Jewish Gnosticism, Merkavah Mysticism and Talmudic Tradition;* Gruenwald, *Apocalyptic and Merkavah Mysticism.*

14. Martha Himmelfarb, *Ascent to Heaven in Jewish and Christian Apocalypses* (New York: Oxford University Press, 1993).

15. Christopher Rowland, *The Open Heaven: A Study of Apocalyptic in Judaism and Early Christianity* (New York: Crossroad, 1982).

16. Haran, *Temples and Temple-Service in Ancient Israel.*

17. St. Benedict, *The Rule of St. Benedict in English,* ed. Timothy Fry (Collegeville, Minn.: Liturgical Press, 1982), p. 47.

18. Marsh, *The Book of Hierotheos*, p. 35.

19. Ibid., pp. 35–36.

20. Ibid., pp. 36–37.

21. Ibid., p. 37.

22. Isaac of Nineveh, *Mystical Treatises by Isaac of Nineveh: Translated from Bedjan's Syriac Text with an Introduction and Registers,* trans. A. J. Wensinck, Verhandelingen der Koninklijke Akademie van Wetenschappen te Amsterdam Afdeeling Letterkunde, Nieuwe Reeks, Deel 22 no. 1. (Amsterdam: Koninklijke Akademie van Wetenschappen, 1923), pp. 10–11.

23. Marsh, *The Book of Hierotheos*, p. 38.

24. Ibid., pp. 38–39.

25. Ibid., 39.

26. Ibid., pp. 40–41.

27. Ibid., p. 42.

28. Ibid., p. 44.

29. Ibid., p. 45.

30. Ibid., p. 46.

31. Ibid., pp. 46–47.

32. Ibid., pp. 47–48.

33. Ibid., p. 47.

34. Ibid., pp. 48-49.

35. Ibid., p. 49.

36. Ibid., p. 50.

37. Ibid.

38. Ibid., pp. 50–51.

39. Ibid., pp. 51, 54.

40. Ibid., p. 55.

41. Ibid., 56.

42. Ibid.

43. Ibid., p. 60.

44. Ibid., pp. 60–61.

45. Ibid., pp. 64–65.

46. Ibid., pp. 65, 67.

47. Ibid., pp. 75–76.

48. Ibid., p. 78.

49. Ibid.

50. Ibid., p. 85.

51. Ibid., p. 133.

52. Ibid.

53. Ibid., pp. 83–84.

Chapter 7: Medieval Rabbinic Authorities

1. Maurice P. Crosland, *Historical Studies in the Language of Chemistry* (1962; rpt. New York: Dover Publications, 1978).

2. "Saadiah (ben Joseph) Gaon," in *Encyclopaedia Judaica* (Jerusalem: Keter; New York: Macmillan, 1971), vol. 14, pp. 544–55.

3. Saadia Gaon, *The Book of Beliefs and Opinions*, introductory treatise, chapter 6; trans. Samuel Rosenblatt (New Haven: Yale University Press, 1948), pp. 29–30.

4. Ibid., treatise 7, chapter 2; p. 265.

5. Ibid.; p. 266.

6. Ibid.

7. Ibid.; pp. 266–67.

8. Ibid., treatise 2, chapter 12; pp. 129–30.

9. Ibid., treatise 6, chapter 7; pp. 255–56.

10. Berakhot 28b.

11. "Rashi," in *Encyclopaedia Judaica*, vol. 13, pp. 1557–65.

12. The translation is my own. For the Hebrew text and less literal translations, see: *Chumash: With Targum Onkelos, Haphtaroth, and Rashi's Commentary, Shemoth*, trans. Rabbi A. M. Silbermann, with Rev. M. Rosenbaum (1934; rpt. Jerusalem: Feldheim Publishers Ltd., 5745); Rabbi Yisrael Isser Zvi Herczeg, with Rabbi Yaakov Petroff & Rabbi Yoseph Kamenetsky, *The Torah: With Rashi's Commentary Translated, Annotated, and Elucidated, Shemos/Exodus* (Brooklyn, N.Y.: Mesorah Publications, 1994).

13. Geo Widengren, *The Ascension of the Apostle and the Heavenly Book*, Uppsala Universitets Arsskrift 7 (Uppsala: A.-B. Lundequistska Bokhandeln, 1950).

14. "Maimonides, Moses," in *Encyclopaedia Judaica* vol. 11, pp. 754–81.

15. On Maimonides's esotericism, see Leo Strauss, *Persecution and the Art of Writing* (Glencoe, Il.: Free Press, 1952; rpt. Westport, Conn.: Greenwood Press, 1973) pp. 38–94; idem, "How to Begin to Study *The Guide of the Perplexed*," in Moses Maimonides, *The Guide For the Perplexed*, trans. Shlomo Pines, 2 vols. (Chicago: University of Chicago Press, 1963), vol.1., pp. xi–lvi; Marvin Fox, *Interpreting Maimonides: Studies in Methodology, Metaphysics, and Moral Philosophy* (Chicago: University of Chicago Press, 1990), pp. 47–66; Aviezer Ravitzky, "The Secrets of the Guide to the Perplexed: Between the Thirteenth and the Twentieth Centuries," in Isadore Twersky, ed., *Studies in Maimonides* (Cambridge: Harvard University Press, 1990), pp. 159–207; David Bakan, *Maimonides on Prophecy: A Commentary on Selected Chapters of The Guide of the Perplexed* (Northvale, N.J.: Jason Aronson, 1991).

16. Elliot R. Wolfson, "Merkavah Traditions in Philosophical Garb: Judah Halevi Reconsidered," *Proceedings of the American Academy for Jewish Research* 57 (1990–1991), p. 183.

17. Maimonides, *Guide For the Perplexed*, trans. Shlomo Pines, 1.19, pp. 45–46.

18. Ibid., 3.24, p. 497.

19. Ibid., trans., 497–98.

20. Ibid.; pp. 498.

21. Ibid.

22. Ibid., pp. 499.

23. Ibid., p. 501.

24. Babylonian Talmud, Shabbat, 55a.

25. Ivan G. Marcus, *Piety and Society: The Jewish Pietists of Medieval Germany* (Leiden: E. J. Brill, 1981).

26. Menahem Mansoor, in Bahya ben Joseph Ibn Paquda, *The Book of Direction to the Duties of the Heart*, trans. Menahem Mansoor with Sara Arenson and Shoshana Dannhauser (London: Routledge & Kegan Paul, 1973), p. 10.

27. Obadyah b. Abraham b. Moses Maimonides, *The Treatise of the Pool: Al-Maqala al-Hawdiyya*, ed. & trans. Paul Fenton (London: Octagon Press, 1981), pp. 82–83.

Chapter 8: Saint Bernard of Clairvaux

1. Jean Leclercq, *Bernard of Clairvaux and the Cistercian Spirit*, trans. Claire Lavoie (Kalamazoo, Mich.: Cistercian Publications, 1976), pp. 15–16.

2. St. Bernard of Clairvaux, *On the Song of Songs I*, trans. Kilian Walsh (Kalamazoo, Mich.: Cistercian Publications, 1971); idem, *On the Song of Songs II*, trans. Kilian Walsh (Kalamazoo, Mich.: Cistercian Publications, 1976); idem, *On the Song of Songs III*, trans. Kilian Walsh & Irene M. Edmonds (Kalamazoo, Mich.: Cistercian Publications, 1979); idem, *On the Song of Songs IV*, trans. Irene M. Edmonds (Kalamazoo, Mich.: Cistercian Publications, 1980).

3. Bernard, *On the Song of Songs I*, Sermon 1:1, p.1.

4. Dadisho Katraya, "A Treatise on Solitude," trans. A. J. Wensinck, *Woodbrooke Studies* 7 (1934): 70–143; texts cited: 136, 139–41.

5. Isaac of Nineveh, *Mystical Treatises,* p. 10–11, 150–51, 328, 365–66.

6. Bernard, *On the Song of Songs III,* sermon 52:3–4, pp. 52–53.

7. Bernard McGinn, *The Growth of Mysticism: Gregory the Great through the Twelfth Century* (New York: Crossroad, 1994), p. 206, noted that St. Bernard intended the condition that later mystics termed a binding or "ligature."

8. Bernard, *On the Song of Songs III,* sermon 52:5.

9. Bernard, *On the Song of Songs I,* sermon 52:5, p 43.

10. Bernard, *On the Song of Songs II,* sermon 7:7, p. 128.

11. Sermon 31:5.

12. Sermon 41:3, p. 206–207; see also sermon 41:4, p. 207.

13. Bernard, *On the Song of Songs III,* sermon 54:2, p. 70; Bernard, *On the Song of Songs II,* sermon 45:6, p. 236.

14. Fazlur Rahman, *Prophecy in Islam: Philosophy and Orthodoxy* (London: George Allen & Unwin, 1958); William M. Brinner, "Prophets and Prophecy in the Islamic and Jewish Traditions," in William M. Brinner & Stephen D. Ricks, eds., *Papers Presented at the Institute for Islamic-Judaic Studies, Center for Judaic Studies, University of Denver Studies in Islamic and Judaic Traditions, vol. 2:* (Atlanta, Ga.: Scholars Press, 1989), pp. 63–82; Harry Austryn Wolfson, "Hallevi and Maimonides on Prophecy," *Jewish Quarterly Review* 32, no. 4 (1942): 345–70, and 33, no. 1 (1942): 49–82; rpt. in: *Studies in the History and Philosophy of Religion,* ed. Isadore Twersky & George H. Williams (Cambridge: Harvard University Press, 1977), vol. 2, pp. 60–119; Alvin Jay Reines, *Maimonides and Abrabanel on Prophecy* (Cincinnati: Hebrew Union College Press, 1970); David R. Blumenthal, "Maimonides' Intellectualist Mysticism and the Superiority of the Prophecy of Moses," *Studies in Medieval Culture* 10 (1977): 51–68; rpt. in *Approaches to Judaism in Medieval Times,* ed. David R. Blumenthal (Chico, Calif.: Scholars Press, 1984); David Bakan, *Maimonides on Prophecy: A Commentary on Selected Chapters of The Guide of the Perplexed* (Northvale, N.J.: Jason Aronson, 1991); Abraham J. Heschel, *Prophetic Inspiration after the Prophets: Maimonides and Other Medieval Authorities,* ed. Morris Faierstein (Hoboken, N.J.: Ktav Publishing House, 1996).

15. Because the Master Mason (Third) Degree of Freemasonry bears a striking resemblance to the Mystery of the Cross—among other details, the responsibility of mind, soul, and body for the initiate's ecstatic death compares with the responsibility of the Jubelo, Jubela, and Jubelum for the death of Hiram Abiff—it may be pertinent that Masonic legend maintains that Hugh de Payens founded the Knights Templar after having made certain secret mystical discoveries concerning Solomon's temple on the Temple Mount in Jerusalem. It is not impossible that the Masonic legend is a fabulization of the historical transmission of the Mystery of the Cross.

16. Bernard, *Treatises* vol. 3, *On Grace and Free Choice*, trans. Daniel O'Donovan, *In Praise of the New Knighthood*, trans. Conrad Greenia (Kalamazoo, Mich.: Cistercian Publications, 1977), p. 115.

17. J. Richard, "Le milieu familial," in Bernard de Clairvaux, *Commission d'Histoire de l'Ordre de Citeau* (Paris: Alsatia, 1953), pp. 13–14.

18. Bernard, *Treatises* vol. 3, p. 138 n. 1; Hans Eberhard Mayer, *The Crusades*, trans. John Gillingham (New York: Oxford University Press, 1972), p. 82.

19. Ibid., pp. 96–98.

20. Peter Partner, *The Murdered Magicians: The Templars and their Myth* (Oxford: Oxford University Press, 1982), p. 10.

Chapter 9: The Holy Grail

1. Geoffrey of Monmouth, *The History of the Kings of Britain*, trans. Lewis Thorpe (Harmondsworth, England: Penguin Books Ltd., 1966).

2. Among competing hypotheses, I have been favorably impressed by Graham Phillips and Martin Keatman, *King Arthur: The True Story* (London: Century Random House, 1992). Arthur is seen as a title of a descendent of the historical Cunneda, who was active shortly after the withdrawal of the Roman legions in 401.

3. Chrétien de Troyes, *Perceval, or The Story of the Grail*, trans. Ruth Harwood Cline (Athens, Ga.: University of Georgia Press, 1985).

4. Roger Sherman Loomis, *The Grail: From Celtic Myth to Christian Symbol* (Cardiff: University of Wales Press; New York: Columbia University Press; rpt. Princeton: Princeton University Press, 1991).

5. Roger Sherman Loomis, "The Origin of the Grail Legends," in Roger Sherman Loomis, ed., *Arthurian Literature in the Middle Ages: A Collaborative History* (Oxford: Clarendon Press, 1959), pp. 276–77.

6. Ibid., p. 294.

7. Ibid., p. 280.

8. Ibid., pp. 288–89.

9. Arthur Machen, *The Glorious Mystery* (Chicago: Covici-McGee Co., 1924), p. 25.

10. Ibid., pp. 38–39, 48. If we use the *Parzival* as evidence that the Knights Templar were privy to the mystery of the Grail, we must still question whether their version of the mystery was the customary one. Wolfram's *Parzival*, alone among the Grail stories, syncretized the Grail with the krater or "mixing-bowl" of Hermetism; see Henry Kahane and Renée Kahane, with Angelina Pietrangeli, *The Krater and the Grail: Hermetic Sources of the Parzival* (Urbana, Ill.: University of Illinois Press, 1965).

11. Leonardo Olschki, *The Grail Castle and Its Mysteries*, trans. J. A. Scott (Berkeley: University of California Press, 1966), speculated that the heterodoxy in question was the religious dualism of the Cathars; but his case rested on a single equivocal motif. In both Chrétien and Wolfram, the Grail radiates light; but since the gospel of John 1:9 describes Jesus as light, there is no basis for interpolating Manichean ideas about light. What is more, current research indicates that the dualism of the Cathars was not a persistence of Manicheism, but an independent departure from Roman Catholic teachings.

12. Philip Schaff and Henry Wace, eds., *The Nicene and Post-Nicene Fathers*, second series, vol. 8, *St. Basil: Letters and Selected Works* (Rpt. Albany, Ore: Sage Software, 1996), p. 548; idem, *The Nicene and Post-Nicene Fathers*, first series, vol. 1, *The Confessions and Letters of Augustine, with a Sketch of His Life and Work* (Rpt. Albany, Ore.: Sage Software, 1996), p. 581.

13. Eugene J. Weinraub, *Chrétien's Jewish Grail: A New Investigation of the Imagery and Significance of Chrétien de Troyes's Grail Episode Based Upon Medieval Hebraic Sources*, North Carolina Studies in the Romance Languages and Literatures (Chapel Hill: U.N.C. Department of Romance Languages, 1976), pp. 52–77.

14. Peter Abelard, *Patrologia Latina*, 77.325; as cited in Esra Shereshevsky, *Rashi: The Man and His World* (Northvale, N.J.: Jason Aronson, 1996), p. 64.

15. Shereshevsky, *Rashi*, pp. 120–29. For access in Troyes to knowledge of Sephardic custom, see Weinraub, *Chrétien's Jewish Grail*, pp.78–87.

16. P. M. Matarasso, trans., *The Quest of the Holy Grail* (Harmondsworth, England: Penguin Books Ltd., 1969). For a discussion of its Cistercian character, see Etienne Gilson, "La Mystique de la Grace dans la Queste del Saint Graal," *Les Idées et les Lettres* (Paris: Librairie Philosophique J. Vrin, 1955), pp. 59–91.

17. Matarasso, *Quest of the Holy Grail*, pp. 43–44.

18. Ibid., p. 274.

19. Ibid.

20. Ibid., p. 275.

21. Ibid., pp. 275–76.

22. Ibid., p. 276.

23. Isabel Mary, "The Knights of God: Citeaux and the Quest of the Holy Grail," in Benedicta Ward, ed., *The Influence of Saint Bernard: Anglican Essays* (Oxford: SLG Press, 1976), pp. 53–88.

24. Helaine Newstead, *Bran the Blessed in Arthurian Romance* (New York: Columbia University Press, 1939).

25. Patrick K. Ford, trans., *The Mabinogi and Other Medieval Welsh Tales* (Berkeley: University of California Press, 1977), pp. 69–70.

26. Arthur Edward Waite, *The Holy Grail: The Galahad Quest in the Arthurian Literature* (1933; rpt. New Hyde Park, N.Y.: University Books, 1961), p. 317.

27. Mircea Eliade, *Shamanism: Archaic Techniques of Ecstasy*, trans. Willard R. Trask (New York: Bollingen Foundation, 1964; rpt. Princeton: Princeton University Press, 1972), pp. 41, 43, 44n, 50, 282, 446; Vilmos Dioszegi, *Tracing Shamans in Siberia: The Story of an Ethnographical Research Expedition* (Oosterhout, Netherlands: Anthropological Publications, 1968), pp. 60–62.

28. Tom Cowan, *Fire in the Head: Shamanism and the Celtic Spirit* (San Francisco: HarperSanFrancisco, 1993).

29. Eliade, *Rites and Symbols of Initiation*, p. 84.

30. Ford, *Mabinogi*, p. 163.

31. Ibid., p. 186.

32. Myles Dillon, *Early Irish Literature* (Chicago, 1948), pp. 101–23.

33. Loomis, "Origin," p. 282.

34. Dan Merkur, *Becoming Half Hidden: Shamanism and Initiation Among the Inuit,* 2nd ed. (New York: Garland Publishing, 1992), pp. 277–85, 290.

35. Loomis, *Grail,* p. 50.

36. Merkur, *Becoming Half Hidden,* pp. 231–300.

37. Glyn Roberts, "Wales on the Eve of the Norman Conquest," in A. J. Roderick, ed., *Wales through the Ages,* vol. 1, *From the Earliest Times to 1485* (Swansea: Christopher Davies, 1959), pp. 78–79.

38. William Rees, "The Norman Conquest," in Roderick, ed., *Wales through the Ages,* vol. 1, p. 82.

39. Ceri W. Lewis, "The Court Poets: Their Function, Status and Craft," in A. O. H. Jarman & Gwilym Rees Hughes, eds., *A Guide to Welsh Literature,* vol. 1 (Swansea: Christopher Davies, 1976), pp. 126–127.

40. Glyn E. Jones, "Early Prose: The Mabinogi," in Jarman and Hughes, eds., *A Guide to Welsh Literature,* vol. 1, p. 191.

41. Ibid., p. 193.

42. *The Song of Roland,* trans. Robert Harrison (New York: New American Library, 1970), p. 13.

43. Thomas Jones, ed. & trans., *Brut Y Tywysogyon, or The Chronicle of the Princes: Red Book of Hergest Version* (Cardiff: University of Wales Press, 1955), p. 31.

44. Ford, *Mabinogi,* pp. 17–19.

45. A. O. H. Jarman, "The Welsh Myrddin Poems," in *Arthurian Literature in the Middle Ages: A Collaborative History,* ed. Roger Sherman Loomis (Oxford: Clarendon Press, 1959), pp. 20–21. The Welsh practice of prophetism is securely dated as early as the ninth century; see Sir Ifor Williams, *Armes Prydein: The Prophecy of Britain. From the Book of Taliesin,* trans. Rachel Bromwich (Dublin: Dublin Institute for Advanced Studies, 1972). It is possible that because of the limitation of extant sources it is widely attested as a popular folkloristic practice only after the twelfth-century transition; see Juliette Wood, "Prophecy in Middle Welsh Tradition," in Hilda Ellis Davidson, ed., *The Seer: in Celtic and Other Traditions* (Edinburgh: John Donald Publishers Ltd., 1989), pp. 52–65.

46. Eliade, *Shamanism,* pp. 33–66; Merkur, *Becoming Half Hidden,* pp. 19–62; Roger N. Walsh, "The Making of a Shaman: Calling, Training, and Culmination," *Journal of Humanistic Psychology* 34, no. 3 (1994): 7–30; idem, "The Psychological Health of Shamans: A Reevaluation," *Journal of American Academy of Religion* 65, no. 1 (1997); 101–24.

47. Jarman, "Welsh Myrddin Poems," p. 46.

48. Ibid., p. 21.

49. Ibid., p. 22.

50. Saint Secundinus, "Hymn on St. Patrick," trans. Ludwig Bieler, *The Works of St. Patrick* (New York: Newman Press, 1953), pp. 57–58.

51. Ibid., p. 62.

52. Ibid., pp. 63–64.

53. Eusebius, *Praeparatio Evangelica* 11.6; Jerome, *In Isa.* 1.1; Augustine, *Enarr. in Ps.* 75.2; 97.3; etc.

Chapter 10: The Kabbalah

1. All translations of the *Bahir* are my own and based on the critical edition of Daniel Abrams, *The Book Bahir: An Edition Based on the Earliest Manuscripts* (Los Angeles: Cherub Press, 1994).

2. Cf. A. C. Lloyd, *The Anatomy of Neoplatonism* (Oxford: Clarendon Press, 1990), p. 126: "The hypostases *are* experiences; they are types of consciousness; while, therefore, they have abstract and objective properties, they have also what we call phenomenological properties."

3. Seth Lance Brody, "Human Hands Dwell in Heavenly Heights: Worship and Mystical Experience in Thirteenth-Century Kabbalah" (Ph.D. diss., University of Pennsylvania, 1991), p. 438. For the Hebrew text, see Gershom G. Scholem, *Ha-Kabbalah be-Provens: Hug Ha-Ravad u-Veno R. Yitzhak Sagi Nahor* (Jerusalem: Akademon, 1963), appendix 1, lines 15–16.

4. Scholem, *Jewish Gnosticism, Merkavah Mysticism and Talmudic Tradition;* Gruenwald, *Apocalyptic and Merkavah Mysticism;* Merkur, *Gnosis,* pp. 155–80; Elliot R. Wolfson, "*Yeridah la-Merkavah*: Typology of Ecstasy and Enthronement in Ancient Jewish Mysticism," in R. A. Herrera, ed., *Mystics of the Book: Themes, Topics, and Typologies* (New York: Peter Lang, 1993), pp. 13–44.

5. Saadia Gaon, *Book of Beliefs and Opinions,* pp. 255–56.

6. Gershom G. Scholem, *Origins of the Kabbalah,* trans. Allan Arkus, ed. R. J. Zwi Werblowsky (Princeton: Jewish Publication Society-Princeton University Press, 1987), p. 55. For the midrashic version, see *Pirke De Rabbi Eliezer: The Chapters of Rabbi Eliezer the Great,* trans. Gerald Friedlander (1916; rpt. New York: Sepher-Hermon Press, 1981), pp. 94–96.

7. Merkur, *Ecstatic Imagination,* pp. 38–39.

8. Scholem, *Origins of the Kabbalah,* p. 132.

9. Joseph Dan, ed., *The Early Kabbalah,* texts trans. Ronald C. Kiener (New York: Paulist Press, 1986), p. 67.

10. Gershom G. Scholem, "The Concept of Kawwanah in the Early Kabbalah" (1934), in Alfred Jospe, ed., *Studies in Jewish Thought: An Anthology of German Jewish Scholarship* (Detroit: Wayne State University Press, 1981), pp. 162–180.

11. Scholem, *Origins of the Kabbalah,* p. 195.

12. Lloyd, *Anatomy of Neoplatonism,* p. 126.

13. Scholem, *Origins of the Kabbalah,* p. 56 n. 12.

14. Daniel Chanan Matt, trans., *Zohar: The Book of Enlightenment* (New York: Paulist Press, 1983), pp. 3–4.

15. Zohar 61b Beshalakh; as translated in *The Zohar,* trans. Harry Sperling, Maurice Simon, and Dr. Paul P. Levertoff, (1934; rpt. London: Soncino Press, 1978), pp. 3, 192.

Appendix: The Belief-Legend

1. William R. Bascom, "The Forms of Folklore: Prose Narratives," *Journal of American Folk-Lore* 78 (1965): 3–20.

2. Carl Gustav von Sydow, *Selected Papers on Folklore* (Copenhagen: Rosenkilde & Bagger, 1948), pp. 60–88.

3. Lauri Honko, *Geisterglaube in Ingermanland,* FF Communications, 185 (Helsinki: Academia Scientiarum Fennica, 1962); idem, "Memorates and the Study of Folk Beliefs," *Journal of the Folklore Institute* 1 (1964): 5–19.

4. Linda Degh & Andrew Vazsonyi, "The Memorate and the Proto-Memorate," *Journal of American Folk-Lore* 87 (1974): 225–39.

5. My remarks here slightly modify and augment the theoretic position of Lauri Honko.

6. The practice of modernizing a traditional teaching without changing the name of the teacher will, I suggest, also help to explain the literary convention of pseudepigraphy in the Hebrew Bible, the New Testament, and both Jewish and Christian pseudepigrapha. Fidelity to a traditional teaching required its continuous upkeep. To preserve a teaching's original form, so that it lost both relevance and adherents, was to falsify its import. For the message to be preserved, the narrative that was its vehicle had to be renovated.

7. Patrick B. Mullen, "The Relationship of Legend and Folk Belief," *Journal of American Folk-Lore* 84 (1971): 406–13; Stanley H. Brandes, "The Creation of a Mexican Memorate," *Journal of American Folk-Lore* 87 (1974): 162–64.

8. Maarti Haavio, *Vainamoinen: Eternal Sage*, FF Communications, 144 (Helsinki: Academia Scientiarum Fennica, 1952).

9. Åke Hultkrantz, *The North American Indian Orpheus Tradition: A Contribution to Comparative Religion* (Stockholm: Ethnographical Museum of Sweden, 1957).

10. Merkur, *Becoming Half Hidden*, pp. 169–200; idem, *Powers Which We Do Not Know*, pp. 174–84.

11. Maimonides, *Guide of the Perplexed*, vol. 2, p. 404.

Index of
Biblical Citations

General Index